Reclaiming Ezer

Reclaiming Ezer

*A Call to Restore and Embrace
Your True Superpower*

STEPHANIE J. BERNARD
LOGAN H. BERNARD

RESOURCE *Publications* • Eugene, Oregon

RECLAIMING EZER
A Call to Restore and Embrace Your True Superpower

Resource Publications
An Imprint of Wipf and Stock Publishers
199 W. 8th Ave., Suite 3
Eugene, OR 97401

www.wipfandstock.com

PAPERBACK ISBN: 979-8-3852-4548-2
HARDCOVER ISBN: 979-8-3852-4549-9
EBOOK ISBN: 979-8-3852-4550-5

01/06/26

. . . we have so great a cloud of witnesses surrounding us . . .
HEBREWS 12:1

To all those who walk unapologetically in their authentic
power and greatness, knowing that it was bestowed
upon them by none other than the Creator.

To my mom and all the *ezer* (עֵזֶר) women in my
life, women who have shaped me, inspired me,
and guided me by their spirit and example.

To my beautiful daughter, who I pray always understands
her God-given value, purpose, and power. I pray that she
uses that knowledge to change the world for the better
and that her acknowledgement of her purpose and power
gives those around her permission to step into theirs too.

Contents

CONTENTS

Preface

Blessed is a person who finds wisdom,
And one who obtains understanding.
For her profit is better than the profit of silver,
And her produce better than gold.
She is more precious than jewels,
And nothing you desire compares with her.
Long life is in her right hand;
In her left hand are riches and honor.
Her ways are pleasant ways,
And all her paths are peace.
She is a tree of life to those who take hold of her,
And happy are those who hold on to her.

PROVERBS 3:13–18

TO MY BEAUTIFUL DAUGHTER,

On September 16, 2008, God blessed me with the opportunity to bring life into this world for the first time. I had prayed relentlessly for a child, and in God's infinite wisdom and abiding love, he sent me you. Becoming a mom and recognizing my responsibility to nurture and cultivate another life was humbling, to say the least, but also an honor like none other. As I peered at you then and wondered who you would become, I could not help but be concerned about the world you would now face. With all of the dangers front of mind, I regrettably became the over-protective parent doing everything in my power to shield you from every bump and bruise to your body and psyche, learning very quickly that this task was an impossible one. It became clear almost instantly that I didn't have all of the answers and that I needed a higher power source to tackle the enormous mission at hand.

As I grow older, I become more and more cognizant of this higher power source and increasingly more dependent upon it. I realize the importance of allowing this higher power to shape our minds, our thoughts, and our beliefs. I recognize our keen ability to perceive and interpret life through the lens we choose, whether viewing the world through carnal eyes or spiritual ones. Such choices are vital, as our mindset dictates every course of action and every path we take in life, for as a person "thinks . . . so he is" (Proverbs 23:7). My favorite scripture, Philippians 4:8, speaks to the importance of focusing our thoughts on things that are "right . . . pure . . . commendable . . . and worthy of praise." These words showcase the need for deliberate, intentional effort aimed at ensuring that our views and attitudes are rooted in the richest soil possible so that we can bear the best fruit.

Even with the best self-help books at my disposal, numerous degrees, and mentors offering advice along the way, I have learned through the years that there is nothing like the ultimate guide, wisdom—from only it comes the highest gain. The book of Proverbs speaks to the essential nature of wisdom, the priceless ability to use God's guidance to translate the best knowledge and understanding into good decisions. It speaks to the importance of using his Word to discern the best actions in any given circumstance. The great author and Nobel Laureate Toni Morrison often told her students not to be content with simply being happy or feeling good in life. She maintained that life must ultimately be about so much more— the "acquisition of knowledge and the hope of wisdom."[1]

---

1. Deray Mckesson (@iamderay), "Don't settle for happiness," Instagram, September 7, 2025, https://www.instagram.com/ reel/DOgWqCfjd3z/

Proverbs, the quintessential model of wisdom literature, opens with a parent encouraging their child to acquire wisdom through Godly instruction and correction. The writer goes on to further illuminate the foundation of this wisdom, reinforcing that, ultimately, it is the Lord who grants it, and thus, it is incumbent upon us to seek it with all fervor as we would the most precious metals, priceless jewels, or valued treasures. He continues by asserting that the best way to search for wisdom is through God's Word and that from it comes true "knowledge and understanding" (Proverbs 2:6). This showcases, ultimately, that the beginning of all wisdom is an enduring, genuine respect and regard for the Lord's way (Proverbs 9:10).

In the world we live in, with all of its ways that are often contrary to God's, wisdom is increasingly a nonnegotiable navigation tool, especially for women of faith. Women today are bombarded with images of what society deems beautiful or popular and guided by what will get the most "likes" on social media platforms or gain acceptance in social circles. Many of the images propagated are not real but take on a form of realism simply due to our repeated exposure to them. Unfortunately, this frequent contact often leaves us numb to the effects of these images, rendering us completely oblivious to the ensuing harm. Many of these images have shaped and contorted our views of women in ways we fail to comprehend.

In light of this reality, on the following pages, I seek to counter such images and the messages surrounding them, hoping to facilitate a search for deeper knowledge and understanding of true womanhood. This work was born out of a sincere concern about the pressures on women to succumb to the worldview and as pushback to the way women are often perceived and portrayed in society. I am particularly concerned about how such depictions impact the perceptions of women of faith. Oftentimes, it seems as if the world has more influence over the views of God's people than the other way around. Although we have been called to be in this world but not of this world, to be a peculiar or strange people, it often seems impossible to distinguish us from the rest of the crowd (John 17:15–16; 1 Peter 2:9). We blend in seamlessly, with no noticeable demarcation in view. We take on the worldview without any thought to how it is completely antithetical to everything God represents. It seems as if we have been so indoctrinated with the world's belief system that God's way and his design is not even seen as the ideal anymore or even viable in practice. I, regrettably, have fallen prey to this mindset myself at times. Sadly, even on the best of days, it often appears that God's perfect plans are only considered meager options among a myriad of mediocre, man-made solutions to man-made problems.

I often wonder, what would happen if we started taking our cues from God instead of trusting our own mindset? What if we endeavored to seek diligently a clearer understanding of God's views and used that as a metric for what we believe and how we behave? I wonder what the outcome would be if we refused to be "conformed to this world, but . . . transformed" by a renewed mind (Romans 12:2). If we fail to do this, I fear we may risk chasing every trend and newfound concept promoted by the culture while missing the boat entirely, never understanding the truth about who we as women are to God. This awareness is essential for all, but especially for young women who are beginning their journey into womanhood and striving to figure out how best to maneuver in these unprecedented times.

These uncharted waters make Lady Wisdom all the more necessary because it calls us not only to greater knowledge and understanding, but greater application of that knowledge to radically transform our thought processes and actions. I hope this book can be a stepping-stone towards greater awareness and insight about womanhood, providing practical ways we, as women of faith, have in the past and continue to live on purpose. I hope it invites deep introspection and honest examination of our beliefs and how they can translate into meaningful action. I hope it empowers us all to truly live out our faith, not just to hear, memorize, or recite the Word but to embody it, for we know that by doing this, we will be like:

*. . .a tree firmly planted by streams of water, which yields
its fruit in its season, and its leaf does not wither; and in
whatever he does, he prospers.*
Psalm 1:2–3

My prayer to you is that as you walk into this precious space
of womanhood, you walk with your shoulders back, head high,
and your eyes and mind focused on what truly matters in life. I
pray that you remain firmly rooted and anchored in an identity
instilled in you by the Creator and that you never allow this world,
or anyone in it, to cause you to doubt your value, question your
purpose, dim your light, or take you off the God-given path he has
tailor-made just for you.

With all my love, Mom

The World's View

*There is a way which seems right to a person,
but its end is the way of death.*

PROVERBS 14:12

PART ONE

The Box That Binds

"The rise and fall of nations may be traced by studying the rise and fall of womanhood . . . A nation can maintain a moral strength no greater than the homes which constitute it, and the home usually rises no higher than the ideals of the woman in it."

—LOTTIE BETH HOBBS[1]

1. Hobbs, *Daughters of Eve*, 3.

Introduction

"But God . . ."

My mom, similar to many of us, served as my first introduction to womanhood. Although she took on this massive charge impeccably, it was not because she had the benefit of experiencing this gift herself. Unlike me, she was never afforded the privilege of knowing her own biological mother. She died when my mom was just one year old. Tragic as it was, my mom somehow was able to endure, although I believe through very little effort on her part.

I hear about God's providence all the time, but it's rare to see it in full form, with such clarity and precision. I stand in awe at what my mom became despite the hapless cards she was dealt, in spite of the treacherous waters surrounding her, and the crushing odds dropped at her meager doorstep. So many others around her, with much less stacked against them, drowned in a far less murky mire, unable to break from the ubiquitous pull, the overwhelming stench, and the unyielding sludge that this world often provides. Although it engulfed many, my mother remained afloat. There's nothing else to attribute it to—but God.

My mom came out relatively unscathed, at least from the outside looking in, but she still had her personal struggles. She grew up in a loving household with two adoptive parents who were anchored in their faith and cared for and supported her. There was no question that God's hand was undoubtedly on her, but the loss of her mother and the gaping hole it left behind still followed my mom throughout her life. She spent many years on a gallant quest for purpose and direction where it seemed there was none, traveling down a road in constant search of the right path, and for her proper place in the world. Luckily, her biological mother had the foresight before she passed, or perhaps was moved through divine intervention, to place her in the care of my adoptive grandmother —a woman of faith who could provide a powerful illustration of what true womanhood looked like when she wasn't able to provide it herself.

It's easy to take for granted the importance of having faithful women in our lives, women who will be that example we all need to help us navigate this rough terrain called life. My mom's story shows us that when we're willing to search, when we're honestly seeking God and his providential wisdom, he always shows up. In Jeremiah 29:13, God says, ". . .you will seek me and find me when you search for me with all your heart." The beauty is that not only does God show up when we seek him, but his abounding grace has a way of providing us exactly what we need at precisely the moment we need it most.

❖ ❖ ❖

And the LORD God said, it is not good that the man should be alone; I will make him a help meet for him.
Genesis 2:18 KJV

While our world seeks to understand and define womanhood using cultural staples, the greatest books, and brilliant minds, the Bible, through the story of creation, perhaps sets the best stage for articulating God's original intent for women. God's ultimate design for womanhood is woven throughout the scriptures but is uniquely described in Genesis, the Book of Beginnings. After God created man from the dust of the ground, it became clear that his creation was not complete, that Adam was not good until he was provided with Eve. The Bible does not explicitly state in Genesis

2:18 what Adam lacked, whether companionship alone or if he had some deeper need. However, the term *help meet* used in scripture may provide some hints.

The word to describe Eve as a help meet is translated from *ezer* (עֵזֶר) in Hebrew and is defined as a helper, ally, or aid.[2] The concept *ezer* is used in approximately twenty-one verses in the Old Testament—the majority of those times referring to God himself as rescuer of his people. As I learned of this word and all it signified, I began to wonder why God would apply the same term he used to identify himself as a rescuer also to describe his creation of women. I contemplated what this terminology may actually communicate about God's original design for women and how that characterization played out in the lives of women in Bible times and applies even to women still today.

In a world where women are often marginalized and sanctioned to stay in their place, where women are often relegated to second-class status, I embarked on a journey of deep reflection and evaluation to disentangle the world's myths and shed light on the truths about womanhood, as defined by the Creator himself. I went on a mission to dispel current ideologies, common notions, and false beliefs working "against the knowledge of God . . . " (2 Corinthians 10:5–6). Although my hope is that this book serves as a catalyst for greater understanding and appreciation among everyone of women's worth, I also recognize the essentiality of women specifically having a deeper awareness of their God-given purpose and value. Thus, this book is also an effort to enlighten and free women, especially from those often-unspoken beliefs hidden in the recesses of our minds, intimating our lack or seeming weakness. This work is an effort to clear a path for women to become more of who God originally purposed us to be.

This is a love letter to all women, young and old, paying homage to those who came before and paying it forward to those currently in the midst or embarking on womanhood today. My

---

2. Strong, *Strong's Expanded Exhaustive Concordance of the Bible*, s.v. "help meet" (H5828).

desire is that this work challenges us all to reclaim our *ezer* nature and embody all that God intended us to be in the first place, as he formed Eve in the Garden of Eden on that blessed sixth day. My wish is that all women will grow to recognize, embrace, and continuously develop their true *ezer* qualities. By doing this, we will empower young girls and women of all ages to tap into their God-given superpowers—powers that can transform their lives and the entire world.

QUESTIONS TO CONSIDER:

1. Discuss some of the experiences you have had with women of strong faith. How have these experiences made an impact on your life?

2. Why is it so important to seek guidance from the Word of God when understanding womanhood?

3. Why do you think God used the same term *ezer* to describe women as he used to describe himself? What do you think this says about how God sees women?

4. What do you think the term *ezer* says about God's original intent or purpose for creating Eve?

5. What does God providing Eve to Adam say about how God cares for his creation?

Walking in Wisdom

When we seek God and his wisdom wholeheartedly,
he always supplies, offering us exactly what
we need when we need it most.

CHAPTER 1

In the Rearview

REMEMBERING THE WAY WE WERE

I THINK BACK TO my early childhood when life seemed much simpler to navigate and easier to comprehend. It was a time when the women in my life played prominent yet unassuming roles, taking on seemingly menial tasks and tackling them seamlessly while pushing through those greater, monumental challenges with grace and tenacity. My mother led the pack, channeling the spirit of the women she had witnessed before her who took on the world without flinching.

My mom was adopted as a baby into a family of powerful women—mother, grandmother, aunts—all strong in their own right. All were rooted and grounded in their faith; each of them committed to giving of themselves in ways that always inspired me. They were women who used every bit of the time they had on earth to fulfill their God-given purpose. My adoptive grandmother, affectionately known as "Nannie," after taking my mother in at one year of age, later adopted two other children from the neighborhood, my mom's twin siblings. She accomplished all this while raising her own biological daughter. Nannie seemed to do it all, taking care of everybody around her. My mother, without hesitation, quickly followed her lead.

Although my recollection of Nannie is minimal because I was so young, there is no question, based on the descriptions of her from others, that I see her spirit living on through my mother. She unwaveringly grabbed the baton when Nannie couldn't carry it any longer, and she ran with it. I recall my mother caring for those around her in much of the same way Nannie had. This was especially apparent in how she cared for my cousins like they were her own. This was evident at all times, but especially on special occasions like Easter or Christmas. My mom would do everything to make those days special for them, buying everyone Easter baskets or presents, or spending time doing my cousins' hair and buying them outfits so that they could look their best when she took them all to church that Sunday. This may seem minor, but with the seven kids my aunt had on top of me and my sister, this was no small achievement. She spent every weekend making sure everyone in the family was taken care of. This care was extended even further when Nannie had a stroke and lay in a coma for months in a nursing home facility. I will never forget sitting by her bedside week after week as a little girl, watching my mother comb and brush her hair, checking on her religiously, without fail, making every effort to ensure she was cared for in the most loving way. My mother's love and concern radiated—traveling to spaces far beyond their source. I don't think even she recognized how much of an impact she made on so many lives. She was just emulating the same behavior she had seen modeled before her.

This same love and care was even extended beyond our family to the wider community. It was clear that my mother was committed to making the world better. She spent the better part of forty years counseling individuals with mental health issues and drug and alcohol addiction. I don't think it was by accident that she landed in such a profession. Alcohol abuse, in particular, was rampant in our family and community. Although she rarely mentioned it, I'm sure watching the impact of addiction on her own family fueled her passion for this work in so many ways. I suspect one of her biggest regrets was not being able to save those closest to her from the detrimental effects of this disease. Despite this, her commitment to helping people live healthy, fulfilling lives was, without question, her calling. I recall as a child wondering how my mother could do it all, and it often was overwhelming to witness. But I can honestly say I wanted nothing more than to be just like her, one who loved God and cared for her family and community at all costs, depositing goodness into every soul she touched.

MY GREATEST FEAR

That type of woman, I fear, is becoming more and more elusive. It appears she's been overtaken by another image—a female no longer identified by her desire to assist those around her in becoming their better selves and a woman with minimal concern for the lessons she leaves behind. It often seems that women today are more worried about achieving their own goals at the expense of setting those around them up for greater success. This altered state is signified by a woman concerned more with individual gain, a woman consumed with the unspoken rule of getting what she feels she is rightfully due instead of ensuring she is depositing valuable nuggets into the next generation so that a legacy lives on long after she is gone.

Selfish ambition appears to rule the day for everyone, taking on a precedent that cannot be denied. I fear such ambition seeks to overrule much of what, perhaps, is of true merit in life. I, by no means, seek to belittle the importance of self-actualization or to minimize the beauty of upward mobility and success. Nor do I uplift the idea of putting your dreams, your livelihood, and well-being in jeopardy for the sake of another's. But unfortunately, I fear the quest for worldly success, for a hollow sense of *happiness* in the right now, and a preoccupation with or overinflation of self, have perhaps overshadowed everything we were created to be. This quest may have eclipsed those things of true value in life—service to and love of God, of family, and of community. My worry is that this new paradigm of womanhood may extinguish and make obsolete much of what true womanhood has to offer and what it was intended for in the first place.

The pull of self-importance is not a new concept, nor is it one relegated solely to women. It is, in many ways, human nature and oftentimes has cultural origins as well. In our society, we have placed psychosocial terms such as self-love and self-preservation on pedestals, as if they are the holy grail that we should seek with all our hearts to obtain, at the expense of all else. We don't consider that there could be other ways of thinking and being.

My junior year of college, I had the pleasure of taking a cultural psychology class where I studied Japanese society. This was followed by an opportunity to travel to Japan the following semester and spend six months studying the culture up close. I was amazed at how the Japanese people lived out concepts such as *omoiyari* and *kikubari*, concepts steeped in the importance of finding self or identity in our relation to others.[1] Such concepts promote living out life's purpose with the needs of others front of mind and living a life in constant awareness and consideration of how your actions positively or negatively impact those around you. Seeing these values firsthand in my interactions, it became clear that these ideals are glaringly distinct from those in Westernized cultures that promulgate a focus on individual rights, desires, and happiness instead of the well-being of all. I often wonder which philosophy Jesus would most identify with.

While notions such as self-love and self-preservation in and of themselves are not harmful, what is troubling is that while elevating these philosophies, we simultaneously minimize or negate all together the importance of other ideologies, including Biblical principles such as humility, dying to, or denial of self (Romans 6:6). We often abandon Christian ethics all together in the name of self-preservation. We even misinterpret scriptures such as "love thy neighbor as yourself" (Matthew 22:37–40) to mean it's paramount that we first work on attaining love of self before we can begin to navigate the sphere of loving other people. However,

1. Longhurst, *Omoiyari*, 106.

perhaps this text implies something very different. What we fail to realize is that love of self in this context suggests focusing on our own self-interests, which we often do automatically. But in our misinterpretation, we end up going down the rabbit hole of seeking to engage in behaviors that we have associated with self-love, and we completely disregard the intent of the scripture. What if the scripture instead suggests that we should consider the interests of others in the same manner in which we already promote our own individual interests.[2] Conceivably, the object of focus is not us at all but others. The assumption is that we as human beings, even with all our faults and brokenness, are already wired to seek to preserve and protect self, and thus, need not be commanded to do so.[3]

If we are truly honest, we have to admit that we are constantly consumed with our own thoughts, our own desires, and our own feelings above everything else, even when these thoughts are shrouded in negative emotions such as self-pity and self-doubt. The object of focus is still categorically the self. The Bible says, "no one ever hated his own flesh but nourishes it and cherishes it" (Ephesians 5:29). We unconsciously preserve self at all costs and protect the ego at every turn, even if in the most maladaptive ways.

Have you ever wondered why no one has to teach a newborn baby to cry when it is hungry or wet? Perhaps because they are born with this ability. It is instinctual for a baby to advocate for itself, to cry until its needs are met. And I believe it remains so as the child gets older. However, loving others unconditionally and placing their needs ahead of our own or having an others-centric approach to life is completely foreign to us. It is completely outside of our very nature. Tackling this command requires intentional effort to see things through an entirely different lens, to operate totally outside of our comfort zone. It requires us to embody the very definition of love, as defined by the Creator, which entails engaging in acts devoid of all that is self-seeking (1 Corinthians 13). This may seem like a monumental task to accomplish, but God rarely commands us to do what is already natural for us. If he did, why

2. Guzik, *Study Guide for Matthew 22*, § D2.
3. Henry, *Commentary on Matthew 22*, ch. 22:34–40, III.

would we need him? What brings me comfort, and I hope eases your mind, too, is that I don't believe God is necessarily calling us to love ourselves any less but just to love others a bit more.

The great apostle Paul noted the danger of placing oneself in such high standing, asserting the importance of not thinking of oneself more highly than we should (Romans 12:3). He spoke fervently about the beauty of placing another's needs and concerns above our own. I wonder if perhaps this humble mindset Paul refers to came from a recognition that God's reason for creating us was not simply for us to seek our own happiness or fulfillment, to do what we think is best or most comfortable for us, or even to protect our own rights or freedoms. Possibly, it is not for us to attain a level of seeming success cultivated by the culture or achieve the aspirations fashioned in our own minds. But, instead, maybe this modest mindset is paramount to us finding contentment in living out God's will for our lives (Matthew 6:10) and for us to ultimately pursue his purpose and plans instead of being consumed with chasing our own.

I don't seek to imply that this is easy or to romanticize about the way things were in the past, but sometimes, I wonder if over the years, perhaps we may have lost our way. I wonder if women in previous generations may have had a better grasp of Paul's thinking in ways women today may not. Women have come a long way, have accomplished monumental acts, and made exceptional strides. But what if, along the journey, we inadvertently lost some prized jewels—some precious pearls, some valuable insights that this world could desperately use today? Perhaps it wouldn't hurt to look in the rearview to observe what many women in our past got right and what many women years prior understood was most important. A little retrospection never hurt anybody, right?

Questions to Consider:

1. What are some valuable insights that women in previous generations have held that may be useful in our current times?

2. Read Romans 12:3. Why do you think Paul tells us not to think of ourselves as better than we are? What kind of mindset is he calling us to as Christ's followers?

3. In Philippians 2:3–4 Paul goes on to say, "Do nothing from selfishness or empty conceit, but with humility consider one another as more important than yourselves; do not merely look out for your own personal interests, but also for the interests of others." How should we live out this scripture in a culture where self-love and self-preservation rule the day?

4. Paul culminates the ideas conveyed in Philippians 2:3–4 by showcasing the ultimate example of a humble mindset through Jesus Christ himself. How can we as women follow this pattern as we endeavor to live out God's calling upon our lives?

Walking in Wisdom

Love greater . . .
God is not calling us to love ourselves less
but just to love one another more.

CHAPTER 2

A Futile Climb

A LADDER OF NO CONSEQUENCE

MANY OF THE WAYS in which women operate in today's times, I believe, have been shaped by the images and beliefs promoted in society. Perceptions surrounding women's worth and value have been influenced by portrayals of women, particularly in today's media, especially in music, television, and film. Such images have left a lasting imprint on our minds, and we have, in turn, perhaps subconsciously, embraced them fully in the context of our reality. Although many might say that the average person understands the difference between "art" and reality, I am not sure that is true anymore. It appears that the lines have been forever blurred through phenomena such as reality television shows and incessant exposure to social media, creations that have bombarded us with photoshopped, catfished, and curated lives. I fear that the images propagated have contributed to the shaping of a generation of men and women who have little concept or appreciation for authentic womanhood. And, even worse, I wonder if there is any desire for the truth or if we are forever invested in, wedded to, and intrinsically tied to the lie. We have, in many ways, been cajoled into viewing the world through filtered lenses, ones that often obscure reality altogether and depict women in a less-than-flattering hue.

In 1993, the renowned rapper, poet, and actor, Tupac Shakur, released the song entitled "Keep Ya Head Up."[1] This was, to many, an ode to women forced to navigate the toils of single motherhood, mistreatment, and disrespect. His words, undoubtedly, were impacted by his upbringing, one in which he had front row seats to his mother's struggle to raise him and his sister on her own. Although his words were rooted in his experience, some might say his words were also prophetic. In many ways, he was surely ahead of his time. His lyrics were armed with thought-inducing questions about how we feel about and treat women. He even went as far as to ask us to ponder whether our actions demonstrate that we actually hate women. Tupac followed with a rallying cry to all to replace such seeds of hate with healing, warning that if we fail to do so, an entire generation harboring ill will towards women may take root, and even worse, spread like wildfire.

Fast forward thirty years, and we notice seeds birthing fruit of similar sentiments. On the heels of the *#MeToo* movement, voices such as poet and coach, Ace Metaphor, assert the same notion that perhaps men really don't like women at all, at least beyond what they can provide for them physically or in a child-rearing capacity. He goes on to suggest that few men understand or appreciate the fullness of having a "capable" woman in their lives (Proverbs 31:10–31) or recognize all that such a woman can bring to the table emotionally, intellectually, and spiritually.[2] He then conveys the beauty and necessity of having a partner that provides a source of strength and wisdom, which can be the glue that holds the family unit together, even when the other partner falters.

1. Tupac Shakur, "Keep Ya Head Up," *Strictly 4 My N.I.G.G.A.Z.*, Interscope Records, 1993.

2. Cam Newton, "Ace Admits to Dating Wildly in the Church, Kita Rose Accusations, and Impact of Tonight's Conversation," *Funky Friday Podcast*, April 25, 2025.

Ace Metaphor's words come with the trial of famed hip-hop mogul Sean "P. Diddy" Combs as the backdrop. On September 16, 2024, he was arrested by federal authorities on charges of sex trafficking, racketeering, and engaging in prostitution. He was alleged to have "used the business empire he controlled to sexually abuse and exploit women, as well as to commit other acts of violence and obstruction of justice."[3]

Although he was later acquitted of all charges except transportation to engage in prostitution, his arrest harkens back to the trial of singer R. Kelley, accused and convicted of eerily similar charges in 2022. Many would declare that such behavior is a grave anomaly, that it represents a few bad seeds in an overwhelmingly wholesome crop. I believe that may be true in many respects. However, it is difficult to disentangle these recent events from the vestiges of prior views hinted at by Shakur and others. Perhaps, indeed, multiple things can be true.

I fear there may be something more wreaking beneath the surface, something that may be difficult for us to face. I wonder if some people, in a proud, resolute, yet quiet way, may identify with such men and their treatment of women. I am curious whether some may seek to accomplish similar goals in far more subtle, less threatening, less egregious ways. I often consider the seemingly casual dismissal of a female's opinions or expertise at work or home, under breath comments rating a woman's body parts as she walks by, touching a woman inappropriately, or making overt advances at a woman despite her disinterest. In light of the pervasiveness of such acts, I am somewhat puzzled by the seeming outrage and surprise over these recent events, as if these are not the type of actions that we have all witnessed for many years through songs, music videos, movies, and even in our very lives. We may shrug off our own behavior and those around us as minor in comparison, but if we're really honest, perhaps we should at the very least consider whether the source of the conduct could be the same. Maybe at its

---

3. U.S. Attorney's Office for the Southern District of New York, "Sean Combs Charged in Manhattan Federal Court with Sex Trafficking and Other Federal Offenses."

root is a mindset corroded by hints of objectification, devaluation, and subjugation of women.

Our vibing to the melodies, swaying to the catchy beats, and reciting the provocative lyrics send a message of acquiescence, even if unwittingly. I'm guilty of it too, having listened to the music and viewed the music videos for a better part of my young adult years. However, I cannot overlook the reality that our careless assent is no excuse for the unacceptable behavior propagated, and perhaps, we must all take full responsibility for our role in perpetuating the notion that such conduct is permissible. The reality is that a person does not have to rape or beat a woman to make it abundantly clear how little they respect her. It seeps into every lie emitted and listening ear averted, every disparaging remark and condescending tone, and every foul innuendo and treacherous act committed. It corrupts every mind in its path and is especially adept at inculcating the psyche of our most impressionable—our youth.

I came face-to-face with this grave reality in a conversation with a middle schooler about an upcoming school dance. When asked if he was going to the dance, the sixth-grade boy casually mentioned, "No, I don't have a girlfriend." I asked unassumingly, "Why not just go with your friends?" He went on to say that's what girls do, not boys, and that all the guys he knew had girlfriends. I laughed and expressed my doubts about that seeming fact, and then he went on to say, "Well, we don't really like the girls; we just use them to exert our dominance over other boys."

I paused to let that sit for a minute. Use them? Exert our dominance? I ascertained quickly what he meant. They used females as a tool to elevate their status among their friends. In an instant, every memory from my years as a young girl growing up rushed in like a flood. It all made perfect sense. His words sounded way too familiar not to be true. I must say I was stunned that this was coming from the mouth of an eleven-year-old. He quickly realized the look on my face and then laughed it off as if it were a joke. But as much as I wanted to believe he was joking, that these searing words were said in jest, deep down I was afraid he said exactly what he meant. At even that young age, it appeared that the mindset I feared most had already taken root—a frame of mind in which females were not truly valued but simply viewed as objects to be manipulated and used in pursuit of self-aggrandizement.

To be honest, women have played a significant role in this outcome too. We are not in any way off the hook. We share in the debacle, for they say no one can ride your back if it is not first bent. Lauryn Hill, famed rapper and actress, alluded to such truths in her acclaimed song, "That Thing," where she calls out women who buy into destructive trends and behaviors, engaging in actions that she notes compromise their souls in the name of popularity. We have often allowed ourselves to be placed in positions where we are marginalized and denigrated, whether knowingly or not. We move in unseeming ways to the very music that calls us out of our name, lyrics that reduce us to mere toys on a patriarch's pathological playground. We show up in spaces desperately seeking male attention, a shot at fame, a chance to live the so-called American dream at any and every cost. Much like all involved, our negligence has given birth and sprouted fruit that none of us ever imagined possible.

THE QUESTION OF PURPOSE

Although some of the negative depictions of women in music may be glaringly obvious, if we look at American media as a whole, including in television and film, we have to admit that we have rarely painted the best picture of women or promulgated the greatest models. Just noting the images portrayed in television and film over the years shows this to be true; that womanhood has seldom been depicted in the best light.

As harmless as it seems, the unassuming mother has no trouble introducing her young toddler girl to the helpless damsel in distress who needs a prince to save her, who pines away awaiting the day that her Prince Charming will show up and sweep her off her little feet, as seen in all the old and some recent Disney movies. I cringe at the images of Cinderella and Snow-White longing for rescue as they await their prince's arrival. As girls age from toddlerhood, we watch remnants of this needy Disney princess image transmute into a full-fledged young woman searching for the one to care and nurture her as she leaves the nest, given away by her father to the seemingly best candidate. This phenomenon plays out often when we venture off to college campuses, bombarded with numerous women who have entered institutions for the sole purpose or primary goal of finding a mate, latching onto the star basketball or football player or the burgeoning lawyer or doctor in the first week of school. These women are, unapologetically, on a mission to find their prince, their knight in shining armor.

This image of womanhood further evolves, as seen in numerous portrayals in films over the years, where there is the female character with impeccable curves and no brains, or the trophy wife placed on a pedestal because she meets a superficial standard set by the culture. Women have often been portrayed as weak, gullible, needy creatures incapable of thriving in the world without someone to care for them and meet their every need.

These images in media become even more convoluted when race is at play. Although portrayals of minority women have grown in the media over the years, problematic characterizations still remain. Over the years, while mainstream women were often portrayed as helpless and needy, minority women were often painted in an opposite, but equally oppressive manner. They were depicted as unflinching stalwarts, incapable of feeling pain or discomfort, uniquely built to serve. While many of these representations of women have been shaped by a patriarchal structure in media, many of these views have also been corroborated by scriptures in the Bible that seemingly describe females in a meager fashion—scriptures that, in the wrong hands, take on a misinterpreted view of women that often equates weakness with a lack of mental capacity or moral aptitude. This is evident through such interpretations of the fall of man that elevate Eve's moral weakness above Adam's, even though God is clear in implicating Adam for allowing sin into the garden (Genesis 3:9).

What is somewhat surprising to me is the magnitude at which women have quickly embraced this mindset. Not only men, but women alike, have been indoctrinated with this limited view of themselves. Sometimes, it appears that women have even internalized it to the point that they really believe that this weakened, debilitating state is one that has befallen them. It causes me to wonder, have we as women been so programmed to believe in our diminished competency or become so accustomed to accepting the perception of our feeble ability that we cannot conceptualize our actual power? Are we operating at reduced capacity even though we have been imbued with the aptitude for greatness?

The sad truth of the matter is that often such negative views in the media have even been orchestrated and sanctioned by women themselves, and even those of color. It is disheartening to observe women leading the pack in embracing negative stereotypes, even striving with all intensity to live up to the standards the industry has set for achieving power and success. It is discouraging to watch women celebrating their comeuppance from sordid deeds—taking acting roles that diminish their value, singing songs that reduce themselves to objects, or making money moves but failing to count the everlasting costs. It is unfortunate to see in our current day overindulgence in plastic surgery and other body-altering procedures and an obsession with designer clothes, bags, and cars that we often cannot afford. Such things promoted by the media have become what the culture deems praiseworthy and seen as the gateway to true accomplishment in life. These emblems have blossomed into a billion-dollar industry, paving the way to apparent acceptance in society, with women investing exorbitant amounts of money to maintain the world's manufactured and false sense of beauty and attainment. It seems as if we often spend so much time chasing the favor of others and the superficial machinations of riches and success cultivated by this world, endeavoring without compromise to be accepted and affirmed by society, that we never step back to decipher whether this is all that there is to life. We never ask the question:

Am I living out my true purpose?

As I get older, I recognize increasingly how little time we have here on earth and that we don't have time to waste living outside of purpose. The reality is that when we are on our deathbeds, we will finally be faced with the certainty that we cannot take any of the stuff we accumulated with us. That all of the money and possessions will be doled out to the highest bidder, to all those precious souls left behind. It will not matter what others thought of us, whether they valued our ability or contributions. We will quickly learn that all of the plastic surgery and augmentations to our bodily form to impress others will be forever forgotten. We will face the fact that we will all return to the dust from which we came—that we will experience the same fate as the bodies of those with less than perfect dimensions. At that moment, I doubt we will wish that we had bought more things or that we had made our physiques that much more *flawless*. I bet we will instead only wish we had lived out the purpose for which we were created.

What if we spend our entire lives chasing after things that don't really matter at all, moving up a proverbial ladder of success that is of no consequence in the grand scheme of things? What if the goals and aspirations we have achieved or continue to chase hold no significance to God, the only one whose opinion really matters? How unfortunate that futile climb would be.

Questions to Consider:

1. In what way has the portrayal of womanhood in society, and specifically in the media, evolved over time?

2. How do you believe the characteristics you have seen in portrayals of women over time align or misalign with God's definition of womanhood?

3. When considering how society's portrayal of women, specifically in media, compares to God's views of women, what scriptures would you use to make or support your argument from question 2?

4. How do you think the world's view of beauty and success, specifically, compares to God's perspective?

Walking in Wisdom

Life is all about purpose.
We have been created with a divine destiny;
our job is just to step into it.
God will take it from there.

CHAPTER 3

In Pursuit of a Shero

"An ezer drops everything to save those
in need . . . An ezer is a hero."[1]

—SARAH FISHER (AUTHOR OF HEBREW WORD LESSONS)

SHADOW-MAN

WHEN I WAS A little girl, I was bombarded with images of super-heroes. They were not only in the latest movies, but even in classic TV shows. I would come home after school each day and watch the TV show *Batman and Robin* religiously, followed by my absolute fa-vorite—*Wonder Woman.* The overwhelming majority of shows had male superheroes, with the few female characters often relegated to insignificant sidekicks, such as Bat Girl or antiheroine characters with complex back stories like Cat Woman. I guess it didn't really bother me at the time. I was only a kid, remiss to the subliminal messages perhaps being conveyed surrounding gender norms.

1. Fisher, "Defining the Ezer Woman," https://hebrewwordlessons.com.

Superman movies were considered the top of the tier back when I was growing up in the eighties and nineties. Everyone tuned in to watch the man of steel save the fragile Lois Lane from destruction, movie after movie. Seeing him enter that phone booth and transform into his blazing red suit was a sight to see. It is somewhat comical nowadays that no one ever questioned why Lois never seemed to recognize Superman, even though they worked together daily, or why no one ever tracked his entry and exit from that magical phone booth. But as soon as his transformation occurred, we held on with bated breath because we all knew he was about to do the impossible, flying off into the sunset to fight the bad guys, freeing the innocent and powerless from dreaded doom. He was the one who saved the day every single time; the one who always managed to show up at exactly the perfect moment.

The image of this invincible character was somewhat shattered in 1995 by the tragic accident befalling the acclaimed Superman actor, Christopher Reeve, who had played this iconic role in four movies from 1978 throughout the eighties. A horse-riding accident left him paralyzed from the neck down, leaving many grieving the loss of America's favorite superhero. His superhero persona had won the hearts and minds of so many that it was a huge feat to find someone to fill his massive shoes. This Superman persona had taken over his real-world identity in ways difficult to explain or articulate with words.

There's something about superheroes that speaks to American culture in ways that are hard to capture. Is it the desire that all of us have for ultimate power, the will to do good to others, to save the lives of those in danger? Or is it that hidden desire many have to fly high above the trees, to see the world from a different vantage point than everyone else? I'm not sure, but over the years, the love of superheroes seems to have grown immensely. I've lost count of the number of Spider-Man or Batman films that have been created, to be honest. There's a clear resurgence of such movies in recent years, with multiple superhero films coming to theaters every year. The growth of Marvel characters alone, such as Black Panther, Captain America, and Thor, is remarkable to witness, characters that never saw the light of day, except among die-hard comic book fans, are now in the spotlight. These superheroes are now, by many standards, even more prominent than Superman himself.

But what is a superhero really? And more importantly, what does our obsession with superheroes say about us as a people? Merriam-Webster defines a superhero as "a fictional hero having extraordinary or superhuman powers or an exceptionally skillful or successful person."[2] Dictionary.com goes further, describing a superhero as "a morally righteous hero in a fictional work who possesses extraordinary abilities or supernatural powers and uses them to fight evil."[3] It is interesting that supernatural or superhuman powers, although at the core of what we believe comprises superhero standing, is often coupled with moral aptitude and a desire to utilize this power for good. Perhaps our love of superheroes stems from our self-consuming desire to be extraordinary, to be more than just average, to stand out in a unique and powerful way. Or maybe our love is based on a more selfless, even noble, innate appetite for conquering evil and fighting for good in the world. Conceivably, it's a little bit of both. Or possibly, it's just a shadow of something even greater.

WHO RUNS THE WORLD?

What cannot be overlooked in media and entertainment over the years is the lack of women in leading superhero roles. And ironically, those few female characters portrayed in lead roles in movies and television often seem to have an evil streak, taking on the parts of reviled villains or antiheroes, such as Harley Quinn or the Scarlet Witch. While women have often taken a backseat in the superhero realm, one has been pretty consistent in her preeminence—Wonder Woman. Old reruns of Lynda Carter's rendition of Wonder Woman on her TV show in the seventies and eighties

2. *Merriam-Webster*, s.v. "superhero," accessed January 20, 2025, https://www.merriam-webster.com/superhero.

3. Dictionary.com, s.v. "superhero," accessed January 20, 2025, https://www.dictionary.com/superhero.

were a young girl's dream. Finally, we could see a woman with just as much, or more, power and strength than any man. It was empowering watching her wield her lasso with such finesse, catching the bad guys and giving them the justice they so richly deserved. The resurgence of Wonder Woman in modern years in multiple movies has further spurred a desire to see more women in such powerful roles. Characters like Captain Marvel, Black Widow, and Jessica Jones have joined the ranks of female superheroes commanding the screen as leading ladies. Little by little, society is loosening the reins on women superheroes, recognizing that female characters, just like males, can also accomplish great deeds in the noble pursuit of good over evil, despite some alluding to the contrary.

Now, the flip side of the coin is that although it appears many folks for years refused to embrace the female superhero character, countless others have bought into the superwoman mantra. I always wondered why Supergirl was always the counterpart to Superman instead of Superwoman, but maybe that's because the superwoman characterization was already being used and had taken on a life of its own outside of the comic book space. The idea of the superwoman as one who can juggle a million things seamlessly at once—can raise perfect kids, be a boss on the job, and be the flawless wife all in the span of a day's work—has become in many women's hearts and minds the ideal. I have even heard renowned neurologists speak about women being built for this precise purpose, noting how women's brains are formulated differently from men's, wired to multitask better when compared to men's tendency to compartmentalize. Many women may take on this title of superwoman with a great deal of pride, feeling that, in fact, she's done her duty as a woman by being able to live up to this moniker.

However, this mindset, I believe, may be just as toxic as the opposite view of female insufficiency, placing manufactured expectations on women that may not be possible to fulfill. The image of the woman made of Teflon, so strong, so capable, that nothing can break her, is exhausting at best. It reminds me of the song from the acclaimed 2021 Disney film *Encanto* entitled *Surface*

Pressure, which articulates masterfully the feeling of carrying the world's burdens on your shoulders. The memorable cadence of melodic beats and stirring stanzas pull you in immediately, before bombarding you with cringe-worthy phrases intimating that we must carry it all, that our worth is tied up in our capacity to serve others without bounds.[4] Such sentiments make my heart wrench every time I hear them because, in all honesty, I can't deny their resonance. But despite admitting that such beliefs speak to many women's experiences, I shudder to think we're passing this frame of mind onto our daughters and granddaughters. I often wonder if this mindset has led to far too many women succumbing to the stress of attempting to do it all. As I look back over my life, I cannot refute that several matriarchs in my family left this world far too young, many of them dying long before their partners.

Is this a result of taking on too much? Perhaps. But much like the Christopher Reeve effect, I believe it speaks to a much more profound truth—that regardless of how much we desire to have supernatural strength, how much we strive to do it all, to fix the world's problems and come through and save the day; the reality is we were never designed for this purpose. We are indeed only human, just like Christopher Reeve, even in his beloved Superman persona. We were never meant to perform the supernatural, at least not using our own devices, or to take on the troubles of this world in our own strength or might. There is a God already in existence for that purpose. Perhaps if we rely on his power, we will see amazing things happen.

Questions to Consider:

1. How would you define the term superhero? What does the term represent for you?

2. Why do you think we, as a society, are so in love with the idea of superheroes?

4. Jessica Darrow, "Surface Pressure," *Encanto (Original Motion Picture Soundtrack)*, Walt Disney Records, 2021.

3. Why do you think women have largely been left out of the superhero space until recent years?

4. Why do you think society has been more comfortable with women taking on the superwoman persona?

5. What do you think our love of superheroes says about how we perceive or feel about God?

Walking in Wisdom

Let God be God.
We were never designed to face life's challenges
in our own strength. We just need to connect
to the real power source—our Creator.

God's View

For my thoughts are not your thoughts, nor are your
ways my ways, declares the LORD. For as the heavens
are higher than the earth, so are my ways higher than
your ways and my thoughts than your thoughts.

ISAIAH 55:8–9

PART TWO

God's Fingerprint

When I consider Your heavens, the work of Your fingers, The moon and the stars, which you have ordained; What is man that You take thought of him, And the son of man that You care for him?

PSALMS 8:3–4

CHAPTER 4

The Real Superhero

There is none like the God of Jeshurun,
Who rides the heavens to your help,
and through the skies in His majesty.
The eternal God is a dwelling place,
and underneath are the everlasting arms;
And he drove out the enemy from before you, and said,
'Destroy!'
So Israel dwells in security, the fountain of Jacob secluded,
in a land of grain and new wine;
His heavens also drop down dew.
Blessed are you, O Israel;
Who is like you, a people saved by the Lord,
Who is the shield of your help and the sword of your majesty!
So your enemies will cringe before you,
And you will tread upon their high places.

DEUTERONOMY 33:26–29

No matter how much we dream, no matter how much we buy into the façade of man-made superheroes or the superwoman mantra, these creations are simply figments of someone's vibrant imagination. No matter how much we wish someone could swoop in and save the day or rescue us from those seeking to do us harm, the reality is that these characters can only accomplish so much. They are fallible creatures, frail and fickle images formed to tickle the fancies of the masses. Regardless of how much we want them to exceed our expectations, even superheroes will fail to live up to the mystical standards we have set for them.

Nonetheless, we still flock to the theaters again and again in search of a great rush of excitement spurred by superheroes' brave acts and ongoing battles against wickedness in the world. Surprisingly, even the superheroes we honor and place on pedestals often speak in terms that harken to Biblical expressions. The noted superhero, Stephen Strange, better known as Dr. Strange, often speaks of the importance of having weapons such as faith, truth, and knowledge in his arsenal, likening them to actual tools of war, comparing them to one's armor, sword, and shield.[1] Such words resemble those of Paul in Ephesians as he appeals to Christians to put on the whole armor of God (Ephesians 6:10–18). These words allude to the truth that even superheroes seem to realize, that they do not have the power within themselves alone to defeat evil forces. Even they recognize the fact that they require a greater power source to fight the battles they face.

Maybe, even at the height of their strength, the best superheroes that we can conjure up in our minds will still fall short. I wonder if our obsession with superheroes, our fervent quest to praise those with supernatural qualities and abilities, speaks to a profound yet obscure truth. I wonder if our desire for a commanding force in our lives with the capacity to do the impossible, to take on the bad guys and always win, is really at its core the thing within us all that we fail to acknowledge—a deep-seated longing for God himself.

1. Starlin, "Dr. Strange," *Marvel Shadows & Light*, no. 2.

GOD AS OUR GUIDE AND RELIEF

The term *ezer* is used numerous times in the Old Testament to specifically describe God. He is typically described in this way within the context of the most dire conditions, often providing much-desired relief or succor in life and death circumstances. This is evident in the first reference to God as *ezer* in Exodus 18:4–12 when Moses notes to his father-in-law the way God delivered Israel from the Egyptians' hands. Anyone who has spent any time in a Christian church or who has heard a few Bible stories as a kid has likely heard about the story of Moses, who led the Israelites out of Egyptian bondage. Those who know the story recall the seemingly impossible situation Israel was in as they escaped slavery, hindered, even if only momentarily, by the overwhelming obstacle of the Red Sea. The Red Sea loomed over them as that unconquerable mountain that could not be moved. But then the God of heaven, in his infinite power, parted the waters, guiding Israel through safely onto dry land, with Pharaoh quickly on their heels. The same sea that was Israel's deliverance was Pharaoh's demise, as the waters rushed back in on him and his army, drowning them all after they had witnessed Israel's victory. Moses even uses this miraculous act as a rationale for naming one of his sons Eli-ezer, noting that it was because "The God of my ancestors was my helper, he rescued me from the sword of Pharaoh" (Exodus 18:4). In this instance, God is portrayed as Israel's *ezer* or help and, more specifically, as the one who guided them to safety, rescuing them from Pharaoh's wrath.

GOD AS OUR STRENGTH AND AID

The term *ezer* is also used in the passages of Psalms to reference God, first in Psalms 20:2 as David gets ready for battle. He prays for God's help, particularly for God to strengthen and support him and his army as they embark on a fierce clash, a life and death encounter awaiting them ahead. As this showcases, the term *ezer* in the Bible is often used in a military sense, indicating the provision of needed support during war. This is especially appropriate considering David's many military exploits, and because we, as Christians, often describe ourselves as being in the midst of spiritual warfare (Ephesians 6), not wrestling with flesh and blood but evil in the spiritual realm. *Ezer* is again used in Psalms 89:19 to note God sending help to "one who is mighty," in some translations signified as a warrior. Many believe this is again referring to David seeking assistance as he prepares for battle.

Even beyond the context of traditional warfare, the scriptures in Psalms show that David continually seeks God's strength and power. In Psalm 70:5, David pleads with God for help against his enemies, specifically, those seeking to do him harm and even those endeavoring to kill him. Throughout his life, he endured many ordeals where he found himself running from King Saul. In these life-or-death moments, David describes God as his only relief, his savior and deliverer, and he urges God to hurry and not delay in providing the aid he so desperately needs. It makes sense for a "man after God's own heart" (1 Samuel 13:14), as David is considered, to recognize such a significant power source at his disposal and to seek this vital assistance from the God of heaven in such a determined way. Given his stellar record in battle and his victory over every foe he encountered, these appeals seem to have resulted in the desired outcome. It perhaps follows that we, too, could benefit from doing the same, to solicit God's help in the context of our struggles so that we, too, can be strengthened and readied for battle by the one with all power in his hands.

GOD AS OUR GUARD AND PROTECTOR

In many instances in the Bible, God as *ezer* is also portrayed in the context of protection and preservation. Psalm 33:20 and 115:9–11 use the term *ezer* to describe God as our "help and shield," signifying him as a protector from danger and harm. A shield is defined in Merriam-Webster as "a broad piece of defensive armor carried on the arm" or "something or someone that protects or defends."[2]

2. *Merriam-Webster*, s.v. "shield," accessed January 20, 2025. https://www.merriam-webster.com/shield.

In Biblical times, a shield was a piece of armor that protected an individual in battle from arrows, spears, or anything else used by the enemy to inflict harm. A shield is poised to skillfully block everything intent on not just inflicting minor harm, but also causing death. In Ephesians 6:16, we are called to use the shield of faith for protection in spiritual warfare. It is also ultimately seen as representative of God's divine protection overall.

In all of the scriptures where *ezer* is used to reference God, it is clear that God is portrayed as his people's constant help, especially in the worst conditions. God is depicted as a faithful source of aid, even when his people did not deserve it, even when they did not acknowledge him as the purveyor of their strength and power. Just like in Biblical times, God remains our source of power still today—our ever-present help—our protector, relief, guide, and strength, especially as we fight numerous spiritual battles here on Earth. In Deuteronomy 33:7 and 26, God is portrayed as riding through the heavens, traveling across the sky to provide much-needed help to Israel in fighting against their foes. In these verses, he is described as their only source of help, depended solely upon to assist them in dealing with those warring against them and their cause. God is repeatedly described as one who comes to the aid of his people, the one who, much like a superhero, swoops in and saves the day, making a way of escape or providing the necessary power to endure life's toughest challenges. This was evident when Pharaoh and his forces were hot on Israel's trail and later when King Saul was aiming to destroy David and his army. The difference, however, between God and this world's superheroes is that God never fails—in fact, it is antithetical to his character and his faithfulness to do so. When he comes to save, he always prevails. What better *superhero* could we ask to have in our corner, working on our behalf, fighting every battle we face? For we know that the battle ultimately is not ours but is surely the Lord's (1 Samuel 17:47).

Questions to Consider:

1. What *ezer* qualities or attributes do we see God exhibiting in scripture?

2. What does the description of God as *ezer* say about his character?

3. What does the description of God as *ezer* say about his love for his people?

4. How does the way God is described in scriptures such as Deuteronomy 33:26 compare to how the world depicts superheroes? What are the similarities and differences?

5. How might someone who embodies the term *ezer* be considered a hero?

Walking in Wisdom

At its core, our love of superheroes is perhaps just a deep-seated longing for a true Savior—God himself.

CHAPTER 5

Embodying the Nature of God

A WELCOME ASSET

IT IS INTERESTING THAT it seems difficult, if not impossible, to find instances in the Bible where weakness or subordinate status is applied to the term *ezer*. When describing God, the term *ezer* is always interpreted in a powerful, strong, and mighty sense—a presence that is welcomed with the highest regard and expectancy. When David seeks God's aid, it is done with the utmost appreciation and anticipation of profound relief, an astounding respite that he recognized could not be provided by a better source. God's help is never described as inferior in status or dismissed as unnecessary in any scriptural context. However, so often we associate *ezer* when applied to Eve as minor in nature. We often assume Eve was a mere accessory to Adam, put on and taken off at his convenience, created for the sole purpose of being his glorified administrative assistant, nanny, or maid. It often seems as though we maintain that she was built simply to help him live out his calling from God, as if to convey she has no calling of her own.

I often wonder why Eve is relegated to such a meager status, why she is not viewed as a vital, powerful presence in her own right, made to complement and strengthen Adam and humanity as a whole. Why isn't she seen as an essential part of God's plans being accomplished here on Earth? Instead, it often feels as if Eve is in the shadows, depicted more as an afterthought in the Creation instead of the enormous asset that perhaps she truly is. *Ezer* connotes a form of help that, when received, allows the recipient to accomplish what they could not achieve on their own. It is quite possible that the help Eve provides is not simply optional, discretionary aid to have at one's disposal if needed, but is instead crucial to realizing the calling God has on our lives. Conceivably, it was never intended that man accomplish God's plans for humanity on his own. Oftentimes, we easily forget or willfully dismiss the truth that, for the first time in creation, God highlighted in Genesis 2 what was *not* good in his eyes— "the aloneness of man."[1]

It is also often overlooked that perhaps Eve's greatest asset to Adam and humanity as a whole was evidenced by Paul's words in 1 Timothy 2:15, where he said, ". . . women will be preserved through childbirth—if they continue in faith, love, and sanctity, with moderation." This text alludes to the declaration in Genesis 3:15 that God would "make enemies of [Satan] and the woman, and of [his] offspring and her descendant." This foretells the truth that God would ultimately prove victorious over Satan through the work of Jesus, the Messiah. I do not consider it a minor thing that women were the instruments the Creator chose to birth, and thus, usher Jesus into the world, the one who represents the ultimate form of rescue from our sinful condition. If the Creator perceived women to be of enough value to be used in this manner, how can we view women as vessels of little significance? What better help could mankind seek from women? And what an honor to be chosen as the mechanism through which the hope of salvation was brought into the world. Perhaps cultural mores have minimized the true value of Eve's arrival on the scene. It is possible that society has completely

---

1. Guzik, *Study Guide Genesis 2*, § C1.

obscured the Creator's original desire to bring about that which was *very good* through the fulfillment of Eve's purpose.

THE HIGHEST COMPLEMENT

In Genesis 2:18, the Bible notes that God makes Adam a mate or helper suitable for him. The concept of being suitable is derived from the term *neged* (נֶגֶד) in Hebrew, which means "counterpart, corresponding to, or parallel to."[2] There seems to be no indication of hierarchy when defining this term. In every sense of the word, it seems to imply equal to or complementary in nature. This idea of suitability, when considered in conjunction with the notion of *ezer*, suggests that Eve may have, in fact, embodied a powerful essence, instead of the much-touted feeble spirit often promoted. That she was imbued by the Creator with great ability, operating as a major asset and much-needed source of aid from a vessel complementary, not inferior, to Adam.

For some, this may be a provocative stance, but oftentimes, it appears that our ability to recognize Eve's, and thus women's value, is often stymied by our interpretation or the meanings we attach to the created order depicted in Genesis. I wonder if we, in our human frailty, may seek to place humanity in the context of a familiar power structure, asserting that there is more value or worth placed upon certain people over others. We appear to operate from a zero-sum mentality that pits people against each other—male against female, young against old, and rich against poor. This concept is based on the impression that whatever is gained by one side is lost by the other. We do this in the church, asking questions such as who has more power or value—elders or the preacher? We do it in the family, pitting men against women, a result of the fall, where Eve is left to navigate an antagonistic, tug-of-war power struggle with Adam (Genesis 3:16). We even see it with the Disciples when they argued about which one was most important to the ministry (Mark 9:30–41, Luke 9:46–48).

2. Strong, *Strong's Expanded Exhaustive Concordance of the Bible*, s.v. "neged" (H5048).

It is as if we cannot conceptualize the notion that we operate in a system orchestrated by a God with abundant resources and infinite power—power that is not diminished when accessed simultaneously by many. What a novel construct to contemplate the fact that we all can truly be extraordinary if we tap into this unlimited power source. We seem to marvel at the idea that there is no need to scrap over proverbial breadcrumbs left behind from someone else's triumphs, but that we can relish in the glorious acts God can bring about in all of our lives. The challenge, however, in seeing this truth is that it requires a sincere acknowledgement that we are operating within a power source that is not all our own. It appears that our human desire to be significant, to have great worth in man's eyes, often negates the Creator's power and essence and, perchance, denies the original intent of the divine order. Perhaps the questions we often ask about power are not biblical questions at all. Maybe they have very little overall spiritual significance but only wreak of the desires of the flesh and our immense carnality.

God the Father and the Son speak to this conundrum through their very relationship. In Philippians 2:6–11, Paul speaks of Jesus' submission to the Father. Although he had the same essence and was indeed equal to God the Father, he bowed to his will. In a similar fashion, perhaps women are called to do the same, being equal to men but assuming a posture of submission, taking on the unique roles and responsibilities given to her by God. And likewise, men are to take on the roles and responsibilities given them in submission to Christ, his head. What if there is no hierarchical value or worth attached at all, only distinctions in functions, roles, and responsibilities evidenced by God working through men and women to accomplish their divine assignments?

After the fall from sin, it is clear that both Adam and Eve are in the same boat spiritually, relegated to a place outside the Garden of Eden, destined to die physically, and fated to work to sustain themselves for the rest of their lives on Earth. Their ultimate fates have no hierarchical standing, but both souls are on an equal playing field. However, despite their equal footing spiritually, it is also evident that Eve has a unique purpose or designation, as does

Adam, and it is important to understand the ramifications of these God-given distinctions.

Although Genesis does not go on to describe in detail how *ezer* qualities show up specifically in Eve, one can assume *ezer*, defined in this context, could parallel in many ways the manner in which it is described in other parts of the Bible, including in the depiction of God. The remaining chapters of this book provide some ways I contend *ezer*-like qualities can show up in the lives of women, as portrayed by examples in the Bible and even among women today. I chronicle women who I believe have embodied the term *ezer*, taking on its very nature—exhibiting what I call superpowers. I showcase, specifically, ways in which women's lives exemplify four core superpowers: relieving power, preservation power, guiding power, and elevation power. I believe these powers are God-given gifts and attributes often present in women that can be fully embodied only through the power of the Holy Spirit.

Ultimately, we as human beings are all created in God's image, so we all share in his spirit and in his essence. We all share in the communicable attributes of God, and we are called to exemplify those traits as we fulfill the roles designated for us. Galatians 5:22–23 perhaps best describes the traits that we as Christ's followers should all seek to personify as the Holy Spirit works within us: love, joy, peace, forbearance, kindness, goodness, faithfulness, gentleness, and self-control. These qualities can show up in many ways as we seek to fulfill the specific roles hoisted upon us, esteeming and embracing them to the fullest extent possible, as we embody the true character of the Creator.

Although we may never know fully or definitively God's motivation behind creating Eve, we have his word as a guide. Maybe women were formed originally to provide liberation from Adam's lonely state, or maybe to offer aid in shared fulfillment of the goals and plans God has for humanity. Feasibly, it is a little bit of both. Whatever the reason God saw fit to create women; it would be a shame to live beneath our blessed calling, resolute to live out a far less, even mediocre vocation, substantiated by this world. What if, in the words of Secretary Hilary Clinton, women truly are "the largest untapped reservoir of talent in the world?"[3] It would be an awful shame to allow all of that talent, all of that grit, and all of that power granted to us to go to waste. I contend that we must stand in the space God created for us as *ezer* women. We must fully become all that God intended us to be when he created us. Our families, our communities, the church, and the world are counting on us.

Questions to Consider:

1. How can *ezer* qualities depicting God in scripture also be applied to women? Have we traditionally viewed women in this way? Why or why not?

2. Why do you think women are often viewed as weak and insignificant in nature? What scriptures are often used to support the view that women are subordinate?

3. Do you agree that women are an untapped reservoir of talent? Why or why not?

4. How have you seen *ezer* qualities show up in the lives of women in Biblical times and even today?

5. What are some ways women today can better embrace and cultivate their *ezer* qualities in efforts to bring God glory? What are some ways that women's talents and abilities could be better used to meet God's purpose?

3. Combe, "At the Pinnacle."

Walking in Wisdom

Life is not a zero-sum game.
Another person's success does not lessen your
opportunity for greatness. We all can accomplish amazing
things if we just tap into God's unlimited power.

PART THREE

A Woman's Work

Restoring Your God-Given Superpowers

Your adornment must not be merely the external—braiding the hair, and wearing gold jewelry or putting on dresses; but let it be the hidden person of the heart, with the imperishable quality of a gentle and quiet spirit, which is precious in the sight of God. For in this way in former times the holy women also, who hoped in God, used to adorn themselves . . .

1 PETER 3:3–5

CHAPTER 6

Relieving Power

The power to provide aid and comfort;
to free from burden.

NANNIE

I've been told that my adoptive grandmother played a major role in my early years, watching my cousins and I during the day as toddlers while my mother and father went off to work. I'm sure my grandmother played a substantial role in shaping my early development, aiding me as I learned to talk, learned to walk, and learned the basics of how to function in the world. Although my memory of her is rather spotty, Nannie lives on through poignant stories from my mom, other family members, and friends, describing her overwhelming compassion, warmth, and love. I know she was a great source of relief for my mom, a working mother struggling to juggle it all. It had to be comforting to know that you had no need to worry because your child was in the very best of hands.

Those who knew my grandmother best remember her as the lady in the neighborhood who took care of everybody. If somebody needed something, she found a way to provide it. She and my grandpa had a farm where they grew acres of vegetables, fruit, and pecans, and they had their share of hogs and chickens, too. They had all they needed, even more than they needed, so they gave it away freely to those around them. Between the farm and grandpa's neighborhood store, no one in the community was lacking. With my grandparents teeming with blessings, you couldn't help but notice the overflow spilling out to everyone in their circle. "Thy cup runneth over" was more than a scripture they read, but a reality they lived. I have learned that it is one thing to experience abundance, but it is another thing to commit to a life and spirit of giving abundantly. Nannie had that spirit, one where she gave of herself and her means without limitation.

God's loving spirit showed up in the way Nannie lived and breathed—the way she ran her household, the way she raised her kids and grandkids, and the way she cared for others in the community. God's spirit showed up in her wise counsel in difficult situations and her inventive solutions for everyday problems. To this day, I still recall my mom relying on remedies passed down from her, including con-coctions of cod liver and castor oils for digestive ailments; menthol rubs, honey, and lemon for colds; and Epsom salt baths when aches abounded. Her wisdom, however, didn't end at her home. She wasn't just a caretaker for her biological and three adopted children, but she assumed responsibility for all those around her, providing a home, a place of refuge, and comfort to whoever was in need. It was as if she saw it as her duty, a calling upon her life. She never hesitated for one minute to provide the relief that others so desperately needed. She aimed to aid for as long as God gave her breath to do so. And that she did—taking care of all of us until the day God called her home. I suspect after witnessing the fruits of her valiant labor over so many years, perhaps God felt, "It's time for you to get some relief now."

"We can do no great things, only small things with great love."[1]

—MOTHER TERESA (HUMANITARIAN AND MISSIONARY)

---

1. Hodge, "Mother Teresa on Doing Small Things."

"IF I SPEAK WITH the tongues of mankind and of angels, but do not have love, I have become a noisy gong or a clanging cymbal" (1 Corinthians 13:1). Such words signifying the importance of love resonate as I think back to my days growing up as a youth in the eighties. You could not turn on the TV without seeing tons of infomercials championing various causes, efforts aimed at raising money for those suffering from issues such as world hunger or childhood poverty. Entertainers in multiple genres were attaching themselves to such noble endeavors. We even had songs like "We Are the World," "Another Day in Paradise," and "Man in the Mirror" that called us all to take notice of how we could help those most in need. Almost every day, figures such as Mother Teresa flashed across the TV screen, spotlighting numerous efforts to feed the poor and aid the sick. She seemed to be a symbol of hope in the darkest of times, someone who provided solace in the most dreadful situations people faced. As a child, I didn't really read too much into it, but I always recalled her image in the midst of throngs of people seemingly plagued by various ailments or maladies stemming from what appeared to be a lack of basic needs being met. I would ask, who was this woman, so small in stature but large in persona? How could her selfless acts of kindness and her meek and giving spirit challenge so many hearts to follow her lead? I wondered what motivated her to continually conduct the menial tasks that rarely received accolades but seemed to matter so much to so many.

Her example helped me realize the beauty and power of doing the small things that so often no one pays attention to but could change the world in the long run. It spoke to the power of going about your day just doing the next best thing, knowing that years of following this pattern would lead to a life well lived, a life where your deeds would truly become your monuments. It showcased the beauty of simply coming to someone's aid who is in desperate need of the essentials—food, shelter, healthcare, and companionship—and how that could make all the difference in the world. I have learned how engaging in these types of acts truly demonstrate that you are your sister or brother's keeper and that such efforts identify you as a true follower of God, living out Jesus's heartfelt words to Peter, "if you love me, feed my sheep" (John 21:15–17).

I then had an epiphany. Such deeds could have a far greater significance, a deeper impact than I initially imagined. Such efforts represented a planting of seeds of sorts—seeds that could bring forth eternal fruit. Providing such relief could, in fact, become someone's first encounter with God himself and then become the catalyst for spreading his love, grace, and compassion throughout the nation and the entire world.

THE POWER TO COMFORT AND AID

The desire and act of rendering aid is perhaps believed to be one of the quintessential qualities of a person of faith. The idea of being a servant to others without thought to receiving anything in return, of having an agape type of love—a sacrificial love—is, in today's terms, a radical posture to take on. Having this highest form of love is a calling that Jesus himself lived out masterfully. He declared to his disciples that their identity likewise was wrapped up in loving acts; that by such illustrations of compassion, people would know who his followers truly were (John 13:35). He even appealed to the ones desiring to be great, showcasing that the pathway towards greatness was paved in servanthood (Matthew 20:26–28). He displayed one of the best examples of this servant mindset by washing his disciples' feet, even the person who would eventually betray him, and the others who would deny him multiple times following his capture (John 13:1–5). This selfless act was only superseded later by the ultimate act—his willingness to suffer and die on the cross to sacrifice his own life for our sake. This is indeed the highest form of love and service to another.

One thing I have noticed over the years is that women's nurturing qualities, in many ways, often resemble this servant-type attitude. Although vast geographical distances and enormous cultural variances exist and often separate us as women, such nurturing characteristics seem to transcend such boundaries. When studying abroad in Japan in college, I had the opportunity to live with a host family. Through this experience I got to witness these nurturing characteristics play out in the lives of the women in the household. Despite the language barrier, the mother and grand-mother quickly took me under their wing and assumed the role of caring for me and ensuring I had all that I needed to thrive in my new surroundings. With such attributes often evident in women across cultures, ethnicities, and generational bounds, it is difficult to decipher whether these behaviors are the result of nurture or nature—if such qualities are evident at birth or are cultivated or learned over time. Nevertheless, it appears that rarely do you have to teach a woman how to care for those around her. It often seems to be an innate ability she has been afforded.

Research even shows the benefit of interactions with women. It is not by chance that studies convey that married men live longer, healthier lives than those who are not.[2] Women have a strong de-sire to ensure their loved ones are healthy and cared for, evidenced through loving acts such as providing nourishing meals, encour-aging doctor's visits, and promoting appropriate medication usage and healthy lifestyle changes.[3] Women often take on the primary role of coordinating and maintaining such activities for their loved ones, especially for their children. Some might say this is expressly apparent and expected among women who carry a child for nine months in their womb. But as exemplified by my adoptive grand-mother, this quality can be evident even when biological offspring are not on the receiving end. Some people just have an especially natural tendency to be a source of aid and comfort to whoever hap-pens to be within their grasp.

SERVANT OF NAAMAN'S WIFE

She said to her mistress, "I wish that my master were with the prophet who is in Samaria! Then he would cure him of his leprosy."
II Kings 5:3

---

2. Jia, "Life Expectancy by Marital Status," 1-9.
3. Long, "Hypertension Self-Management," 1000-1006.

Wisdom in Scripture

Naaman was a powerful warrior and captain of the King of Aram's army. Although he was a very highly regarded leader in the Syrian army, he was suffering from the condition of leprosy. This condition started with changes to the skin, and led to hair loss, rotting fingernails and toenails, and eventual death. There was no known cure.

The Arameans had taken a girl captive from Israel, and she had become the servant of Naaman's wife. One day, the girl told his wife that there was a prophet in Samaria who could cure Naaman of his leprosy. She mentioned that this prophet was named Elisha. Upon hearing this, Naaman received permission from the King of Aram to go seek out this prophet, and he traveled and stood in the doorway of Elisha's residence and waited, hoping for relief from his dreaded disease. A messenger came out and told him to "wash in the Jordan seven times, and your flesh will be restored to you and you will be clean" (II Kings 5:10). Naaman could not believe such simple instructions could lead to such profound results, so he resisted profusely until his servants were able to coerce him into submitting to the guidance. He eventually followed the instructions and, to his surprise, was instantly healed.

The beauty of this story is that the servant of Naaman's wife, although a victim of capture and subsequent servitude, still had a heartfelt desire to offer the opportunity for relief to her master, Naaman. Her actions showcased God's ability to use people in all conditions of life to accomplish great deeds. God permitted the calamity of the girl's seizure to achieve a higher good, a higher purpose. Instead of harboring bitterness and hatred from her confinement, the girl still maintained a heart of concern for her master, coupled with a sincere faith that could move mountains.[4] Her declaration showed that she never once doubted that Elisha could cure Naaman, and her immense faith and unwavering concern proved overwhelmingly beneficial, providing great comfort and relief to Naaman and his family.

4. Guzik, *Study Guide for 2 Kings,* § A2.

PHARAOH'S DAUGHTER, MIRIAM, AND JOCHEBED

> *Now the daughter of Pharaoh came down to bathe at the*
> *Nile, with her female attendants walking alongside the*
> *Nile; and she saw the basket among the reeds and sent*
> *her slave woman, and she brought it to her. When she*
> *opened it, she saw the child, and behold, the boy was cry-*
> *ing. And she had pity on him and said, "This is one of the*
> *Hebrews' children."*
> *Exodus 2:5–6*

Someone we rarely discuss in great detail in scripture is Pharaoh's daughter, a woman who is not even identified by name, but merely characterized by her standing in society. She is mentioned solely for discovering and caring for a baby she found traveling along the Nile riverbank, covered by a conspicuous blanket and lying in an intricately woven basket made of papyrus plants, tar, and pitch. Upon discovering the baby, the Bible notes that she names him Moses, signifying that he came from the water. There is no mention of hesitation on her part in deciding to care for him, even as she saw the clear marker of his Hebrew heritage on his covering. Although she was aware, I'm sure, of the edict from Pharaoh to kill the Hebrew boys, she took on the role of caring for him as if he were her very own son.

The actions of Miriam, Moses's sister, should not be overlooked either. At a very young age, she dutifully eyed baby Moses as he traveled down the Nile River, doing her best to ensure that he ended up in safe hands. Once she saw that Pharaoh's daughter found Moses, Miriam wisely went to her and asked if she wanted her to bring a Hebrew woman to nurse him. The Pharaoh's daughter agreed, and Miriam brought Jochebed, Moses's own mother, to the rescue. The blessed irony in this historical account is that Jochebed, in her desperation, had hatched a plan to save her son from death, wanting nothing more than to see him safe and his precious life spared. But because of her overwhelming faith, she ended up with so much more. Not only was his life spared, but he ended up in a house of royalty where he received the highest level of care and protection possible. As if that wasn't enough, the icing on the cake was that Jochebed was even paid by the Pharaoh's daughter to nurse her own son. This allowed her to continue to play a prominent role in his life through his most formative years, offering her the opportunity to instill in him a genuine love of the true God and his chosen people. This is a powerful testament to God's providential hand, as evidenced through the care and aid of his people, and God's willingness to reward the faithful above and beyond measure.

PRISCILLA

> *Now a Jew named Apollos, an Alexandrian by birth, an eloquent man, came to Ephesus; and he was proficient in the Scriptures. This man had been instructed in the way of the Lord; and being fervent in spirit, he was accurately speaking and teaching things about Jesus, being acquainted only with the baptism of John; and he began speaking boldly in the synagogue. But when Priscilla and Aquila heard him, they took him aside and explained the way of God more accurately to him.*
> Acts 18:24–26

Although we often speak of the role women play in helping their spouses and rearing their children, we hear far less about women aiding in other areas of life, such as ministry. In fact, in many instances, the role of women in ministry has been minimized or neglected altogether. Priscilla is touted as one who, along with her husband, was a tremendous asset to furthering Paul's ministry. Paul exhibits great confidence when he leaves Priscilla and Aquilla, this husband-wife duo, in Ephesus to minister and teach the young preacher Apollos (Acts 18:26). Biblical commentators debate why Priscilla was mentioned alongside Aquilla and, on some occasions, named first. It was rare for women to be mentioned at all, let alone ahead of their husbands. Some suggest this could denote her immense knowledge of the Word or her status socially, but either way, there is no question that Priscilla was a true benefit to her husband and to Paul as they endeavored to do God's work. It is evident that both Aquila and Priscilla took Apollos under their wing and played an active role in helping further enhance his understanding of God's way.[5] Although adept in his knowledge and gifted in the teachings of John the Baptist, Apollos profited greatly from this deeper instruction from Priscilla and Aquilla.

Paul called this couple his "fellow workers" in ministry and celebrated them for the work they did in risking their lives for the cause (Romans 16:3). Much of the missionary work Paul was able to do was because of the help he received from co-workers in the faith. Their efforts showcased the beauty of partnering to aid in the fulfillment of God's mission, and the strength that comes only through working hand in hand to accomplish God's purpose. Their union is a striking illustration of the power that only comes through a united front, as shown in scriptures such as Proverbs 27:17: "As iron sharpens iron, so one person sharpens another," or in Ecclesiastes 4:12, "if one can overpower him who is alone, two can resist him."

Priscilla and her husband were a tremendous source of aid and relief to Paul in his ministry, a testament to the way God never calls his people to a mission without equipping them with everything they need to carry it out. Priscilla and Aquilla's example conveys the truth that you can often accomplish far more with help along the way, that as a team, you can go much further than as an individual. It shows that when people lay aside their own ambitions in pursuit of a common cause (2 Corinthians 5:15), it is unimaginable the weight and force of their impact on the work of the Lord.[6]

LIVING ON PURPOSE

All of these women, without hesitation, helped in bringing relief to those around them. Pharaoh's daughter, Miriam, and Jochebed ensured the safety and well-being of Moses and the eventual

5. Baxter, "Priscilla—Acts 18," paragraph 5.
6. Baxter, "Priscilla—Acts 18," paragraph 6.

deliverance of God's people from Egyptian bondage. Naaman's wife's servant facilitated the much-needed comfort that Naaman needed to continue his mission, while Priscilla provided invaluable support and aid in the fulfillment of Paul's ministry. I wonder if these women could even conceptualize that their natural inclination to render aid and relief would end up playing such a monumental role in God's agenda. This speaks to how God can use our unassuming yet purposeful actions to move his immense plans forward.

Questions to Consider:

1. In what ways have you and other women in your life provided aid and relief to those around you?

2. Do you see similarities between the way God provides relief and aid to his people and the way you and others exhibit this quality? If so, in what way? If not, why?

3. Is there a character, male or female, in the Bible that you identify with most that represents how you seek to exhibit the qualities of comforting and aiding those close to you?

4. If God has entrusted you with this power or gift, how can you use it best to bring him glory?

Walking in Wisdom

Consider others more.
Your rendering aid and relief could be someone's first
or only encounter with God.

CHAPTER 7

Preservation Power

The power to guard and protect; to keep from harm or danger.

MOM AND ME

Growing up in the Deep South, I will never forget how my mother had a plethora of superstitions. I was never sure if she fully believed them all or if she just held onto them in the event that they proved true. But either way, it was abundantly clear that we as kids could never talk or move during a thunderstorm, for this was the time when God was doing his best work. We could never open an umbrella indoors or fail to eat black-eyed peas and collard greens first thing on New Year's Day for fear of bad luck and poor earnings all year. Although these traditions were simply man-made and carried very little weight in the grand scheme of things, she also promulgated even more valuable customs over the years that I have held onto religiously. She was, and still remains, a constant prayer warrior. She never failed to pray as the clock struck midnight on New Year's Day or every morning and night thereafter, after she read her scriptures. We rarely missed a Sunday morning church service or Bible study. God was an ever-present force acting throughout our lives. It is not surprising that this force continued to operate as I started my own family.

One can go on and on about the damage done by clinging to superstitious beliefs and practices, and I don't by any means deny the merits of this notion. But there's also no denying that at the root of most, if not all, of my mother's traditions was the desire to preserve and protect what was most precious to her.

As I started my own family, a similar desire to guard and protect what was dear to me evolved into comparable practices, such as the blessing of our homes and blessing of our children in an effort to pray God's goodwill upon all in the household. This sentiment was similarly promoted by strategically placed scriptures throughout the home as reminders of who, in fact, ruled the house. All who dared to enter that edifice was immediately bombarded with phrases such as, "As for me and my house, we will serve the Lord" (Joshua 24:15) and "For I know the plans I have for you . . . plans to prosper and not harm you" (Jeremiah 29:11). Guarding and protecting what God had blessed us with was without question always forefront of mind. We desired to send a clear and resounding message—a cautionary tale—to all that dared to attempt disrupting or dismantling what the Lord had established. That glaring message declared that God is especially adept at taking care of what belongs to him, while simultaneously handling those who work against his people and his cause (1Samuel 17:26–37).

> "We married their mission, and that became our
> mission when they were no longer here."[1]

—CORETTA SCOTT KING

[Statement at the funeral services of Betty Shabazz, referencing her bond with Betty Shabazz and Merlie Evers, wives of slain civil rights leaders Malcolm X and Medgar Evers].

---

1. Chang, "Coretta Scott King and Betty Shabazz".

I HAVE ALWAYS ADMIRED the strength and spirit of Coretta Scott King. Growing up in Atlanta, it was impossible to miss the overwhelming presence of the King legacy. But even in light of the legacy her husband's ministry and mission left on the city, she, too, left an indelible mark that could not be ignored. Her quiet, meek, but powerful persona shone through whenever she walked into a room, whenever she graced the podium, or took the microphone to speak. This power was undeniable, speaking volumes, as could only come from a woman who had endured the worst and come out bruised but not beaten on the other side. The triumphs of a woman who spent the bulk of her adulthood raising a family in the midst of ongoing pain, fears of death, and the resulting agony of loss showcased a power unlike any other. Despite her distress, despite her immense sorrow, she found solace in her sisters, Betty Shabazz and Merlie Evers, who had experienced the same anguish and an all too familiar loss. She found comfort in the cause they all held so dear, that all people would one day be free to live out America's creed that all are truly created equal.

After her husband's assassination, Coretta did not stop fighting but instead found her second wind. She founded the Martin Luther King Jr. Center for Nonviolent Social Change, she fought tirelessly to make Dr. King's birthday a federal holiday, and she endeavored to revitalize the Sweet Auburn district of Atlanta, home to historic Ebenezer Baptist Church and King's boyhood home. In the midst of all these efforts, she continued to bring about the change her husband and others like him had valiantly fought and died for, championing the cause of civil and human rights for all. Together with other women in the movement, she found the strength to continue on, protecting the legacy her husband left behind, while safeguarding her family and maintaining and advancing a collective mission. Without the efforts of Coretta and other women in the Civil Rights movement, and their courage, tenacity, and uncompromising resolve, I doubt their husbands' legacies would be what they are today. These women represent the unyielding power to guard and protect what we as women hold so dear, our loved ones' lives, our families' legacies, and a long-lasting mission to leave the world better than we found it.

THE POWER TO GUARD AND PROTECT

Even nature itself gives us hints at this superpower. I recently read an article about a chimpanzee at the Bioparc Zoo in the Spanish city of Valencia that gave birth to a baby that died a few days later.[2] Although tragic in its own right, the more chilling part was that the mom had been carrying the dead baby around with her for three months and would not let it go. The zookeepers had allowed this to go on in respect for the grieving process, despite how strange the behavior appeared. It was so jarring that they'd had to communicate to patrons why she was clinging to a decaying body for dear life. If nothing else, it speaks to the mother's instinct to preserve and protect her offspring at all costs. We often tell people not to get in the middle of a mama bear protecting her cub. This innate desire and ability to guard and protect our offspring often translates even to humans. I doubt many will argue against the belief that mothers will fight to protect their children, no matter what trouble they have landed in or mistakes they have made. Similarly, wives will fight to keep their families intact, understanding the importance of what God designed and the essential value of every member. Women for generations have done what is required to ensure their family was preserved and protected, understanding the importance of the family unit and everyone's place within it.

Women have also rallied to fight for their communities, understanding that all of its members' "freedoms are shackled" to each other's, in the words of the late Fannie Lou Hamer. This fighting spirit often held by women is masterfully depicted in more literal ways in films like *The Woman King* and *Black Panther*. Such films have, in recent years, showcased women fighting valiantly for their nation and their people. Full of action-packed performances, superhero characters, and inspiring themes, the portrayal of strong

2. Reuters, "Grieving Chimpanzee Carries Dead Baby."

warrior women in such films is unparalleled. These depictions are unprecedented in the film arena but are even more awe-inspiring because they are based on real-life events instead of fiction.

In the seventeenth century, the West African kingdom of Dahomey, now modern-day Benin, rose to prominence under the protection of its all-female military forces. Known by such names as the Agojie or Amazons, they were powerful agents used to defend and guard the Dahomey empire.[3] These women were ready and willing to die in the pursuit of protecting their nation. They were not only great fighters, but expert hunters and gatherers, skilled in archery and growing crops. These women, much like the female characters depicted in today's films, could seemingly conquer the worst obstacles. But what was even more evident by their example is that they understood and embraced their power. They refused to step down or cower in the face of battle. They were more than willing to go to war for what they saw as a worthy cause, and they exuded unimaginable will and fortitude in protecting and guarding what was of most value to them.

I believe that same spirit, that same strength, that same determination, is evident in women during Bible times and is still present today. The only difference is that we wield this power on and off the battlefield using spiritual weapons, with God and his son at the helm. We understand, ultimately, who we are working for, while likewise knowing who we are working against.

In her recent book, "I am Ezer," author Michelle Harrell contends that *ezers* are warriors, and part of holding that title requires you acknowledging and pursuing the true enemy. She maintains that so often we waste precious effort on fighting the people we encounter instead of the true culprit, evil forces bent on taking us off course and taking us off mission. She asserts that there are times in life when we must go toe-to-toe with the forces determined to work against us and the purpose God has for our lives.[4] I think we all can agree with this sentiment, that we, at some point, have to stand face-to-face with and fight the giants in our lives head on.

3. Jones, "Warriors of West African Kingdom."
4. Harrell, *I Am Ezer*.

Ezer, when referring to God, often points to a shield, a form of protection, keeping all things away that wish to do you or your loved ones harm. A shield appropriately represents women as well, individuals who are ready and willing to do what is necessary, defending against anyone and everything set on destroying what belongs to the Lord. Such women continue on in the spirit of David, who, when up against the giant, Goliath, shouted, "Who is this uncircumcised Philistine that he should defy the armies of the living God?" (I Samuel 17:26). These women, much like David, come armed to battle with a tireless faith. It is safe to say that anyone who accepts the challenge of warring against these women and those they are sworn to protect is surely bound for a similar fate as dear ole Goliath (2 Thessalonians 1:6).

SHIPHRAH, PUAH, AND JOCHEBED

> *Then the king of Egypt spoke to the Hebrew midwives, one of whom was named Shiphrah, and the other was named Puah; and he said, "When you are helping the Hebrew women to give birth and see them upon the birthstool, if it is a son, then you shall put him to death; but if it is a daughter, then she shall live." But the midwives feared God, and did not do as the king of Egypt had commanded them, but let the boys live.*
> *Exodus 1:15–17*

Wisdom in Scripture

Several women in the Bible have played prominent roles in preserving and protecting God's people. With the ominous backdrop of Pharaoh's edict that all of the Hebrew boys be killed due to substantial growth in Israel's population, there is a light shining at the end of an otherwise dark, desolate tunnel. This tunnel is guarded by faith-filled, defiant women, intent on operating in constant pursuit of God's aims and plans instead of Pharaoh's. Midwives, such as Puah and Shiphrah, defied the Pharaoh's orders to kill all of the Hebrew males born and instead devised a plan to ensure their survival (Exodus 1:15–17). They feared the Lord more than Pharaoh and despite his instructions to them to make sure all boys born to Hebrew women were murdered, these women made the wise decision to follow God's precepts instead of the current law of the land.

Their efforts were furthered by a Hebrew mother's courageous actions. Jochebed was blessed to give birth to a baby boy in these challenging times, one that she knew had a calling on his life. Despite Pharaoh's orders, she, too, took matters into her own hands and hid him for three months before placing him in a basket and sending him down the Nile River, praying fervently for his safety. We know he was eventually found by the Pharaoh's daughter and raised in the royal household. Each of these women had a firm, unshakeable faith that defied the status quo. They refused to allow fear and doubt to hinder them from protecting and guarding precious life. Their efforts preserved and protected Moses and ensured that the plans of God would not be thwarted, and that the ultimate deliverance of his people would be accomplished.

ABIGAIL

Now there was a man in Maon whose business was in Carmel; and the man was very rich, and he had three thousand sheep and a thousand goats. And it came about while he was shearing his sheep in Carmel (now the man's name was Nabal, and his wife's name was Abigail. And the woman was intelligent and beautiful in appearance, but the man was harsh and evil in his dealings, and he was a Calebite).
1 Samuel 25:2–4

As in Moses's story, faith and tenacity continued in women throughout the Old Testament. Abigail provided a striking example of the power to guard and protect her loved ones. She was married to a man named Nabal, whose name and behavior was synonymous with the term "fool." She was described as a woman of great wisdom and beauty, while he was identified as obstinate and evil in all his ways. In 1 Samuel 25, King David, traveling near Carmel, sent word to Nabal informing him of the great deeds he had done on his behalf over the years, protecting his flock and shepherds from danger. After asserting his goodwill, he requested a return on the favor, asking that Nabal offer provisions to him and his servants. Nabal, in response, foolishly belittled David or snubbed him by saying, "Who is David?" (1 Samuel 25:10). He disrespected him profusely by insinuating David's lack of importance, even though it was well known by all in the land who David was. Everyone knew that he was the future king. When Abigail found out, she quickly rushed into action. She knew that the fate of her family, her entire household, was at stake.

Although she was not aware of David's specific plans, Abigail hastened to gather gifts to offer to David directly to assuage him. David had vowed to slaughter Nabal and his entire family because of the slight towards him, but once Abigail caught up with him, she bowed before him and appealed to his better self, urging him not to take vengeance on them and have blood on his hands. She implied, in a humble yet impactful way, that such action would in no way be pleasing to God or proper for a future King. Abigail also did what most would not. She took credit and responsibility for the wrongs her husband, Nabal, had done, recognizing that when he was in error, the whole family was impacted. She, being a woman of God, in her wisdom, set aside her pride and did what was necessary to save her family. She covered his blight for the sake of her household—doing what she needed to do to fight for and defend what was dear to her and, more importantly, what was of value to God.

DEBORAH

"The Lord, the God of Israel, has indeed commanded, 'Go and march to Mount Tabor, and take with you ten thousand men from the sons of Naphtali and from the sons of Zebulun. I will draw out to you Sisera, the commander

of Jabin's army, with his chariots and his many troops to
the river Kishon, and I will hand him over to you."
Judges 4:6–7

During the period of the Judges, Deborah was also a powerful force in her own right. In these patriarchal times, she served ancient Israel as a prophet and sole female judge, a remarkable accomplishment for a woman. In Judges 4, it became clear that the people of Israel had continued in a familiar pattern of disobedience, and consequently, God, in judgment, turned them over to the Canaanite king, Jabin. Israel had suffered immense persecution from Jabin and the commander of his army, Sisera, for twenty years. Sisera, known for his nine hundred chariots and numerous warriors, mistreated Israel so intensely that they cried out to the Lord for help. Deborah was the one whom the people came to in order to gain Godly insight and guidance, particularly in perilous situations. This communication was a two-way street, with Deborah imparting prophetic words to the people in the midst of their cries.

After hearing from the Lord, Deborah summoned Barak, Israel's military commander, to inform him of the calling God had given him. He was called to rally ten thousand troops and go out against Sisera and his army. Barak was fearful due to the sheer size and might of Sisera's forces. However, Deborah assured him that God had instructed him to go to battle and had promised victory. But his fears overshadowed all God promised, lessening his willingness to do as God commanded, leaving him hesitant and uneasy about the prospect of proceeding. Thus, Barak agreed to go only if Deborah accompanied him. Her response to his reluctance was, "I will certainly go with you; however, the fame shall not be yours on the journey that you are about to take, for the LORD will sell Sisera into the hand of a woman" (Judges 4:9).

Although Deborah assured him that if she went to battle, he would not be crowned victorious and success would fall to a woman, he agreed to this fate. In response, she did not hesitate to go to battle for her people. I imagine God getting the victory was the only thing on her mind. With her leadership and unrelenting determination to fight for Israel, along with God's unlimited power at work, she recognized success was inevitable. In Judges 5:3, Deborah gave credit where it was due for the victory, saying, "I will sing praise to the LORD, the God of Israel!"

LIVING ON PURPOSE

Much like these women in the Old Testament, many women today have that same fighting spirit—they have that can-do attitude that says, I am going to do what God says, no matter what. They hold the belief that fear and insecurities will not hinder them from doing what God has called them to do. They are women who refuse to give up or give in when things get difficult or when tasks seem too overwhelming to conquer, who fight on through the struggle, understanding where their power truly lies.

Most, if not all, of us have women like these in our lives. I see this essence in my own mother, humble by the culture's estimate, but mighty in spirit. I don't think it's by accident that two of her biggest role models growing up were Angela Davis and Shirley Chisholm, two strong fighters in their own right, one fighting for freedom over injustice and the other for political power and advancement. Similar to them, my mom fought her own personal battles—financial struggles, health challenges, and grief from death. She, like Davis and Chisholm, didn't answer to the world's cacophony telling her to give up or to give in, telling her that what lies ahead is too difficult to navigate. She kept pushing despite the pain, despite the disappointment, despite the stress, because she knew there was purpose in all of it. She pushed through, never allowing her faith to bow to the weight of the world's many misfortunes.

Fighting for, protecting, and defending who she was, what she believed in, and those most important to her, has always been in her DNA. She never backed down from a fight, not a worthy one anyway. I learned from her the power of fighting through, through the hurt, through the challenges, through the setbacks, knowing that what's on the other side is more than worth the struggle. She understands, still, that her steadfastness, her dedication, and her commitment benefit those around her, leaving a lasting legacy of faith for generations to come. Just like many women before her, she lives by the powerful words of the song "You Fight On."[5]

Questions to Consider:

1. What role do you or other women in your life play as guardian and protector of those close to you?

2. Is this role representative of the way God guards and protects his people? If so, in what way? If not, why?

3. Is there a character, male or female, in the Bible that you identify with most that represents how you exhibit the qualities of guarding and protecting?

4. If God has entrusted you with this power or gift, how can you use it best to bring him glory?

Walking in Wisdom

Don't cower in the face of life's giants.
Be ready and willing to protect and preserve what is of value,
fighting against forces intent on hindering God's purpose.

---

5. James Pinckney, "You Fight On," *The Sound of Holiness*, OPHIRGOSPEL, 2020.

CHAPTER 8

Guiding Power

*The power to steer or lead towards
a destination or course of action.*

LUCY MAE

They often say, "You may be the only Bible people read." This quote speaks to the commanding energy of influence or the "capacity or power of persons or things to be a compelling force on . . . the actions, behavior, and opinions of others."[1] Perhaps one of our greatest influences as women of faith is our ability to plant seeds, to be individuals who sow seeds that can bring forth the greatest crops imaginable. I'm sure my mom never conceived this would be her reality as she set foot on the campus of Stillman College in the late 1960s. She stepped onto her college campus ready to take on the world. She was the first from her family to go to college and knew everyone back home was praying for her to succeed. She quickly rose to the occasion, tackling her studies with fervor and holding onto her goals and aspirations even tighter. She was headed down a straight pathway to success when she

---

1. Dictionary.com, s.v. "influence," accessed August 10, 2025, https://www.dictionary.com/influence.

met my dad, a sophomore ready to take on the world just like her, bent on succeeding by any means necessary.

It was clear my dad was different from many other guys. This was evident when my mom met him. On that very day, she walked by a group of guys on campus who proceeded to speak to her inappropriately to gain her attention. My dad quickly jumped into action, coming to her aid, confronting the guys, and calling out their negative behavior. It was clear then that he was a man with his own mind, focused just like her on learning and progressing in life and not reveling in foolishness. From then on, she quickly learned that he was also a man of integrity who truly valued family, education, and faith.

As my mom was learning about who he was, similarly, he was taking notes on her, I'm sure. One of the greatest lessons my dad ever learned, perhaps, came from my mom in the coming years. Some might say her influence led him to make one of the greatest decisions of his life, but one cannot deny the power of God to place the right people in our lives at the most opportune moments. Even though my dad had grown up in a religious household, his beliefs differed in many ways from my mom's. Although there was some contention around this fact, my mom's dedication and commitment to her faith won out. I believe it was because she not only spoke the words in the Bible to him, but her actions illuminated them as she shared with him the things she had learned in countless sermons and Bible studies held in her living room as a child. My dad was smart enough to take notice. He later got baptized and married her following graduation. After being baptized, he spent the remainder of his days as a dedicated man of faith.

I watched my mom's influence shape him and our household in ways that are difficult to put into words. I always say she was the spiritual guiding force for us all, a compass directing us in "the Way" (John 14:6; Acts 24:14). My dad embraced her faith, not simply because of the words she spoke, but I believe because of the life she lived. She was the Gospel he had often read and heard preached but had rarely seen brought to life. Her influence was undeniable and harkens to the intent of 1 Peter 3, which speaks of a wife winning

*over her husband by her Godly character. My mom lived this truth,
and our entire family is better because of her lasting influence.*

> *"Let us remember: One book, one pen, one child,
> and one teacher can change the world."*[2]

—MALALA YOUSAFZAI

*(Excerpt from Malala Yousafzai's speech given at the United
Nations Youth Assembly, July 12, 2013, in New York City)*

THESE WORDS NEVER RING truer than when we look at the life
of Malala Yousafzai. Malala witnessed at the young age of eleven
atrocities that many of us can't begin to imagine. In 2008, the Taliban invaded and took control of her city in Pakistan. They forbid
the use of TV and music and severely punished anyone who dared
to go against their edicts, but perhaps the biggest blow was their
prohibition of girls attending school.

Malala was raised by parents who valued education for all
children, including girls. Her father was a noted teacher and sup-
porter of girls' education, and he started a school in their town
when Malala was growing up. He and Malala's mom instilled in
her a love of learning and a strong belief that she and all girls deserved the right to an education. So, despite the Taliban's orders,
Malala refused to forgo her learning, and in October 2012, she was
met with the consequences. She was shot in the head on her way
home from school. Luckily, she survived, but it took many months
to recover. But when she did, she was resolute to take on the world
and, particularly, those who vowed to keep her and other girls
from learning. She finished school and started her own organi-
zation to advocate for the rights of girls to receive an education.
She even became the youngest Nobel laureate, receiving the Nobel
Peace Prize in 2014 for her efforts.

The Taliban recognized what many understand still today that
the way to silence generations is to silence the females one by one.

2. Yousafzai, "United Nations Speech."

What the Taliban didn't realize, however, was that for all the women and girls who would shirk under the pressure, many more were intent on fighting back. The Taliban didn't calculate that there were Malalas throughout the world, willing and determined to beat the odds. Malala expressed this truth boldly when she spoke of the powers that exist in our world—the sword, the pen, and women. She professed proudly that women were the strongest power of them all.[3] Women, the backbone of every family, every society, every community, play an undeniable role in cultivating, nourishing, and nurturing our future. Even Malala's father, Ziauddin Yousafzai, noted in a recent podcast the harm that patriarchy causes to both men and women, contending that communities and nations that fail to honor and support the efforts of their women and girls "walk with one leg."[4] His words denote the essential nature of every member of the body, physically and figuratively, and highlights the need to allow all in society to operate at their fullest capacity. It is clear that women are a powerful force, and through their guiding influence, they are perfectly positioned to help shape the future— to shift the trajectory, to lead us forward, transforming families, communities, and the world for the better.

THE POWER TO INFLUENCE AND TEACH

If anyone were to ask my kids about my long discussions with them regarding faith, society, music, and the list goes on, they would, without question, roll their eyes and let out a resounding sigh in perfect unison. They know all too well that I will make a lesson out of the most mundane things. Many a lofty discussion has come about from a scene in a TV show or movie, or a trivia session will arise from a song that comes on the radio, followed by an offer to give them $5 if they can name the musician or the title of the song. One of my favorite scenes from the 2021 movie *King Richard* is when the main character sits his kids down to watch the classic Disney film, *Cinderella*, to teach them a lesson on humility. Every time he switches off the

3. Yousfazai, *I Am Malala*, 31.

4. Georgetown Institute for Women, Peace, and Security, "Malala Yousafzai's Dad."

TV and asks them, "What did you learn?" my kids cringe as I note for the millionth time, "See, he's just like me!" I believe everything, and I mean everything, can be a teachable moment.

This truth was further validated in an exercise at my church, where all Sunday school teachers were asked to complete a survey on spiritual gifts. Not surprisingly, my top gift was teaching, followed closely by shepherding. Several years later, it was further solidified by receiving the same results on another spiritual gifts survey. I guess, if nothing else, this surely is one of my superpowers. Although teaching is a common role for women, even in the church, oftentimes, shepherding is less so. When we think of the term shepherd, we typically think of someone who tends sheep, either in Biblical times or in rural areas, even today. Some may also think of an individual, often a man, in a church who is charged with guiding and directing the flock or parishioners. Less often do we think of women taking on this role. However, Larry Gilbert, in his book, "How to Find Meaning and Fulfillment Through Understanding the Spiritual Gift Within You," purports that shepherding is defined as meeting the needs of those under your care and coaching or leading them in a certain direction.[5]

Sounds a lot like what women do, doesn't it? Not surprisingly, it is often a gift that is held in conjunction with the gift of teaching. Although these roles are often minimized in women, particularly in the church, it is impossible to deny the fact that women often have a keen ability to guide and to influence those around them. This power, however, much like all things, can be used for good or evil.

EVE AND THE IMMORAL WOMAN

When the woman saw that the tree was good for food, and that it was a delight to the eyes, and that the tree was desirable to make one wise, she took some of its fruit and ate; and she also gave some to her husband with her, and he ate. Genesis 3:6

5. Gilbert, *Team Ministry*, 157.

78

Wisdom in Scripture

We see the use of this guiding power for evil very early in the Bible in the Garden of Eden, where Eve entices Adam to eat of the fruit of the tree that God told him was forbidden. He was not deceived like Eve but willingly took of the fruit at her urging. There's no evidence of him hesitating in this act. I believe this speaks to her incredible influence and her uncanny ability to lure the first man created into defying the voice of the living God.

As a teenager, I watched the old classic movie, *Splendor in the Grass*. The main character, Deanie, struggles with the pressures of maintaining her virtue while navigating the realities of teenage love. Suffering a painful breakup and reckoning with the loss of love to a woman less concerned with propriety was unbearable. On the surface, the other girl seemed to get the much-wanted prize—the charming, handsome guy. But you're left to wonder in the end if there's a far more subliminal message lurking beneath. This film and so many others speak to the faulty view that a woman's power lies primarily in her sexual prowess and her ability to seduce or entice a man. This flawed perspective is, however, challenged in scriptures like Proverbs 5, where a father explicitly warns his son of the dangers of immoral women. Verses 3–4 note that "the lips of an immoral woman are as sweet as honey and her mouth is smoother than oil, but in the end, she is as bitter as poison, as dangerous as a double-edged sword." Solomon speaks about the dangers of this prowess in not only tempting and devouring men, but the certain nature of this prowess in defiling reputations and destroying lives (Proverbs 6:32).

This truth is further portrayed in Proverbs 31:3, when King Lemuel imparts his mother's sage advice to his own son: "Do not give your strength to women, or your ways to that which destroys kings." King Lemuel, in so many words, acknowledges the seductive power women can use to bring about Satan's ends. But his recollection of his mother's wise instructions, I believe, alludes to an even greater truth, that this same influence can be used by women for a far greater purpose, to generate an environment where God's ends are met instead of the enemy's. His mother's guidance created a nourishing environment where faith and obedience could grow and flourish, conveying a woman's power to perceive what's in the best interest of those around her and to chart a path to bring it to fruition. She used her position and influence to promote and preserve what was righteous in God's eyes by providing wise counsel and direction to her son that would equip him for the challenges he and his seed would encounter in the future. His mother's example represents, perhaps, the manner in which God truly calls us as women to use our immense influence—ultimately to lead people to him.

The scriptures in Proverbs remind me of the song "Poison" by the '90s R&B group Bell Biv Devoe. This song notes the misfortune that can come from engaging with the wrong woman and the destruction that can befall a man enticed by the words and behaviors of a woman led by the most unsavory forces. The lyrics speak to this powerful influence women possess, whether they realize it or not, an influence that could instead be used to harness and direct others at all costs towards good. Romans 14:13–19 notes the importance of not causing anyone to stumble, but instead, doing everything in our power to encourage others to good works and to engender a greater faith. Although this responsibility does not fall on women alone, I believe we must do our part to use our influence for positive ends.

Perhaps the best evidence that exists of women's capacity to make the greatest impact through our positive influence can once again be found in the beginning. Despite being deceived by Satan and playing a prominent role in the fall of mankind into sin, women accomplished something far more significant in being utilized by the Creator to help repair the breach, by bringing mankind back into relationship with him through his son (1 Timothy 2:15). As women today, it would be befitting for us to continue this aim, to allow God to work in and through us, so that we never seek to lead people away from God, but always towards him. What a noble charge for us to work to ensure, as best we can, that our actions are not tempting individuals to sin, but always inviting them to righteousness (2 Corinthians 5:18–19).

LOIS, EUNICE, AND HANNAH

She, greatly distressed, prayed to the Lord and wept bit-
terly. And she made a vow and said, "LORD of armies, if
You will indeed look on the affliction of Your bond-servant
and remember me, and not forget Your bond-servant, but
will give Your bond-servant a son, then I will give him to
the LORD all the days of his life, and a razor shall never
come on his head."
1 *Samuel* 1:10–11

Just as a woman's influence can be used for evil, it is exponentially more powerful when it is used for good. Paul showcases women's positive influence in his numerous writings to Timothy. Whenever I read 2 Timothy 1, I am reminded of the incredible strength and power that comes from a woman on a mission to bring about the best in people's lives by leading and guiding them towards what's most important. Lois and Eunice were credited with introducing the great preacher Timothy to the Gospel, the one whom the great Apostle Paul entrusted and charged to carry out his ministry (2 Timothy 4). Paul speaks highly of Timothy's "genuine faith . . . the faith that first filled your grandmother Lois and your mother, Eunice. And I know that same faith continues strong in you" (2 Timothy 1:5).

It is evident that Paul recognized and appreciated the tremendous role these women played in nurturing and facilitating the growth of Timothy's knowledge of the Lord and his strong faith. I imagine for Lois and Eunice, faith was not something to be minimized or taken for granted, which is why they made it such a priority in Timothy's upbringing. This was the case among the women in my family as well. Faith was something to be celebrated and shared with as many people as possible. The influence my mom, adoptive grandmother, and great-grandmother had on my family's faith is undeniable. In many ways, their example of faith played a substantial role in the family's trajectory, ushering in five generations of believers. They say you know a tree by the fruit it bears, and these women set the stage for a glorious harvest. Their knowledge of the scriptures and their willingness to allow them to rule their lives was passed down like the words of the best oral historians, griots, and truth tellers of our time. It was passed down from generation to generation, spreading just as the greatest of traditions and most honorable customs. These women introduced my family and countless others to the Gospel knowingly and un-knowingly. They introduced it through asserting the essentiality of God in everything, in every experience, in every action, in all aspects of their lives. Their example, much like Lois and Eunice's, speaks volumes today about the role women can play in being the first and often primary teacher of Biblical principles to their children and others in their midst, leaving a lasting legacy of faith.

This guiding influence is similarly displayed powerfully in other women in the Bible, such as Hannah, who had so much foresight and faith in God that she committed her son, Samuel, to the Lord even before his conception. I imagine she recognized the immense importance faith had played in her life and would undoubtedly play in her son Samuel's life as well. She never forgot how she prayed fervently to God, and he blessed her with a child, and she never forgot the vow she made to give him back to the Lord. Accordingly, she placed her son, Samuel, on a solid course where living a God-centered existence was not just by happenstance but was non-negotiable. As he came of age, she left him in the care of Eli, the priest, stating that, "for this boy I prayed, and the LORD has given me my petition which I asked of Him. So, I have also dedicated him to the LORD as long as he lives . . . " (1 Samuel 1:27–28).

LIVING ON PURPOSE

Many women today, in their own way, are operating in ways similar to Lois, Eunice, and Hannah, dragging their kids to church services, whether they want to go or not, reading them Bible stories before bed at night, and having deep conversations about faith in the presence of rolling eyes and seemingly closed ears. These are all ways of introducing their children and others to the Lord through actions, even more than words. These women are unfazed and unbothered by their loved ones's disinterest, their imprudence, or dogged resistance. These women understand that guiding their loved ones in cultivating a genuine relationship with the Lord is a unique gift that they are grateful and uniquely empowered and positioned by God to grant to those entrusted to their care.

Questions to Consider:

1. What role do you or other women in your life play as guides and teachers of those close to you?

2. Do you think this role is representative of the way God guides and teaches his people? If so, in what way? If not, why?

3. Is there a character, male or female, in the Bible that you identify with most that represents how you exhibit the qualities of guiding and teaching others?

4. If God has entrusted you with this power or gift, how can you use it best to bring him glory?

Walking in Wisdom

Live the Gospel.
It is often read and preached but rarely brought to life.
Through genuine faith, may your presence make
a God-centered reality non-negotiable.

CHAPTER 9

Elevation Power

The power to raise to a higher level, magnitude, or status; to propel forward or advance.

LUCY HARGROVE

My mother was named after my great-grandmother, Lucy Hargrove. I've been told she was a woman, small in stature, but mighty in presence. She was the kind of woman who walked into a room with her mere 5-foot status and commanded respect, not by her words or speech, but by her character, by a spirit that intimated a value that could only come from the Creator himself. They say you tell people how to treat you by the way you carry yourself, and she did that brilliantly without uttering a word. Everyone in her midst had to rise to the occasion. And when she spoke, everyone listened, knowing that whatever was coming from her mouth would be filled with wisdom.

She was the true matriarch of the family, setting the tone for how everyone else was to operate. Her uncompromising faith was perhaps her greatest attribute. She never ran from the opportunity to showcase her beliefs. She never hesitated to welcome the neighbors into her living room for worship services and Bible studies. She never wavered, once enough money was raised for a church building, to continue to help further the kingdom as a devoted founding member of the local congregation. Her name, to this day, is still listed, along with my grandparents, on the walls of that church building because of her tireless efforts to help engender a space where true spiritual growth could occur. Her aim was to win as many souls for Christ as possible, and she never shied away from that goal. She was deeply committed to her faith, providing a shining example for all to see, especially her namesake, the woman who raised me.

I imagine being in her presence was a call to higher heights, that she elevated everyone around her, beckoning them into a posture of excellence just by the way she presented herself to the world. I imagine witnessing her living in her greatness gave others permission to follow her lead by doing the same. Our family is indebted to her for her example of faith, for leading the charge, for setting the bar so high, and for sending a powerful message that mediocrity is not an option. She showed us that excellence is always within our grasp, for if we reach for the heavens, we'll always end up somewhere in the stars.

"When they go low, we go high."[1]

—MICHELLE OBAMA

(Excerpt from Michelle Obama's speech at the 2016 Democratic National Convention)

IN 1882, JIGORO KANO created the Japanese art form of Judo, also known as the "gentle way."[2] Highly influenced by samurai practices, Kano formed Judo in response to harsh combat styles, such as jiu-jitsu, that historically dominated the Japanese landscape. These earlier martial art forms incorporated moves such as punching, blocking and kicking to subdue an aggressor, techniques that had the primary goal of causing bodily injury and even death to one's opponent. Judo, however, moved away from such techniques

1. Obama, "Democratic National Convention."
2. MMA Conditioning Association, "Complete History of Judo."

that relied solely on force and strength to conquer an opponent, to methods which harnessed and redirected the opponent's momentum, ultimately using it against them. These new methods no longer involved meeting force with greater force, but meeting force with greater principle. Kano's efforts showcased the capacity to observe an opponent's attack strategy and then make a conscious decision to respond in a different way. Kano saw Judo as something higher than just a means of protecting and defending oneself against an enemy, but as a way of life that promoted mutual respect and benefit through the improvement of oneself and others. This new practice masterfully elevated martial artistry by fusing useful defense techniques with the honorable but often underutilized art of compassion.

In her notable speech at the 2016 Democratic National Convention, Michelle Obama took this approach further by coining the term "when they go low, we go high."[3] This speech, supporting then presidential candidate, Hillary Clinton, was in response to the vitriol occurring during the race against Donald Trump. She noted that, "When someone is cruel or acts like a bully, you don't stoop to their level."[4] She spoke to a philosophy that sounded quite similar to ones we have heard many times in the Bible, represented by phrases such as "turn the other cheek" (Matthew 5:39) or "love thine enemies" (Matthew 5:43–44). All of these scriptures speak to the idea of not being consumed by evil but overcoming evil with good (Romans 12:21). I love that the First Lady called us to this higher stance, appealing to our best selves instead of our worst.

The prophet, Nehemiah, took a similar approach when he was attacked for rebuilding the walls of Jerusalem. His response to his critics was, "I am doing a great work and am unable to come down" (Nehemiah 6:3). So often, however, we are quick to stoop to the levels of those around us, to get back at them for what they have done to wrong us, to render evil for evil. We say things like you have to fight people in a language they understand, or that certain people just won't respond to acts of kindness or love. There

3. Obama, "Democratic National Convention."
4. Obama, "Democratic National Convention."

may be some truth to that idea in the short run, but I am not convinced that lowering our standards to align with the world's ever pays off in the long run. Perhaps, we serve a God who calls us to so much more. Perhaps, we serve a God who challenges us to consider the long game.

We could use more people like Jigoro Kano and Michelle Obama calling us to higher ideals, elevating our thinking, strengthening our resolve to do and be better than what we may see in front of us, to use our power, as the Bible says, to truly "provoke unto love and good works" (Hebrews 10:24). I appreciate such individuals who understand that hate and vitriol do what they do best: breed, spread, and multiply. Only the opposite force has any chance of bringing such evil to a complete and total halt.

This is especially important, as another great orator, Martin Luther King Jr., alluded to many years ago. He noted that it is impossible for darkness to extinguish darkness, that only light has the capacity to accomplish such results.[5] This philosophy mirrors the intent of John 1:5 which states: "the light shines in the darkness, and the darkness did not comprehend it." Dr. King equates this analogy to hatred, landing ultimately with the truth that only the stronger, opposing force—love—can effectively address this ill. His words and the principles underlying them are just as profound and relevant today as they were the day he uttered them almost seventy years ago.

THE POWER TO UPLIFT AND STRENGTHEN

When I think of the power of strengthening and uplifting people, I automatically think of the analogy of propping someone up, helping them reach their highest potential, or helping them rise to an elevated level. It reminds me of a sort of stepping stool or a helping hand, providing the backing one needs to move up a little higher to the next echelon. If we are lucky, we have people in our lives who not only provide us with an example of the greatness we

5. King, "Loving Your Enemies."

could achieve, but also dare to give us a little nudge, encouraging us to take the steps to attain it. We often aim to do this with our kids, often being resolved to the notion of providing a better life for them than we had or seeking to leave a legacy that positions them for success, but we do it less so with other people.

This reminds me of an instance in the Bible, in Exodus, when Amalek came to fight against Israel, and as long as their leader, Moses, held his staff up, Israel triumphed. But when Moses's hands grew weary, Aaron and Hur stepped in to support them so they wouldn't fall, "one on one side and one on the other." (Exodus 17:8–13). Israel ultimately prevailed with the help of the two brothers propping Moses' arms up, keeping them at the highest level possible so that victory was assured. May we all be so lucky to have Aarons and Hurs in our lives, helping us to excel and accomplish great things in life.

Unfortunately, though, so often it seems we diminish the concept of support to someone helping us stay in a stagnant stance instead of someone inspiring us to aim higher. We relegate support to the idea of someone accepting us in our current state or agreeing with our current position, regardless of whether it's where God wants us to be. It is human nature to want to be accepted by others and not judged, but sometimes, I wonder if we often place acceptance on such a high pedestal that we accept things about ourselves and those around us that perhaps we should not. It is true that God has not called his followers to condemn or hypocritically judge anyone, but instead to the greatest gesture—love. What we often fail to recognize, though, is that real love, although patient and kind, also gently nudges and restores those who falter or may be traversing down a destructive path (Galatians 6:1).

It was clear in Exodus that God maintained that if Moses's hands stayed high, Israel would be victorious. Similarly, God has set standards for our well-being to ensure our victory, but so often, we get tired, rebellious, and oftentimes complacent. We, just like Moses, may need someone nearby who is willing and able to step in and strengthen and support us when we are weak, when we fall short, as we all will at some point in time. It's what they often call accountability partners, those we can go to who will tell us the truth about ourselves, whether we want to hear it or not. Those individuals are the ones who love us enough to tell us the things that will help us live better lives and not simply feel better in our own mess.

On the surface, it may seem ideal to surround ourselves with those who will allow our proverbial hands to fall because it's comfortable resting on our own laurels and allowing ourselves to become content with where we are in life. It appears ideal because it doesn't require either party to put forth any effort to change or to grow. However, this assumes the posture that we are meant to be stagnant figures content with never growing or progressing in our faith or in life. Fallen rapper, Nipsy Hussle, maintained that if the ones in your circle of influence are not inspiring you and motivating you to reach higher levels, then perhaps you don't possess a circle at all, but instead a cage. I wonder if many of us are stuck in a prison of our own making because we have not taken the opportunity to surround ourselves with greatness, failing to recognize that the most successful people are not exceptional in their own right, but are elevated by the talents and gifts of those around them. Perhaps God intended us all to be on a constant journey towards spiritual growth and development so that elevation occurs among those around us. Paul said to think of others as greater than ourselves, speaking to the concept of humility. The beauty of this notion is that if everyone thinks of everyone as higher than self, then everyone is uplifted, and no one is looked down upon.[6] Michelle Obama similarly noted that individuals who are really strong are in the business of exalting, exhorting, and lifting people up. What a wonderful world it would be if we all lived by this golden rule.

The idea of having such a force in one's life played out in an altercation between the famed actor, Jonathan Majors, and his now ex-girlfriend. Jonathan Majors alluded to the idea of not being content with their relationship, suggesting that he deserved a higher caliber mate, one who would be what he called his Michelle Obama or Coretta Scott King. Although his statement reeked of entitlement and an overly inflated perception of self, I wonder if

6. Guzik, *Study Guide Philippians 2*, § A2.

his mindset may reflect many people's thought process. Both of the women he mentioned were brilliant and gifted in their own right before they met their spouses, Michelle, an accomplished attorney, and Coretta, a trained musician. I am sure Dr. King and President Obama both appreciated the many gifts and insights these women brought to the table. Many even say these great men married up and became greater men because of it.

Although I don't agree with Majors's statement or the chauvinistic tone underlying it, I understand and have heard many times the same sentiment from other men. When I was younger, everyone, similarly, said they wanted their Claire Huxtable, the wife and mother from the acclaimed *The Cosby Show*. She was an intelligent, powerful boss in her own right, willing to speak her mind, even to her husband. Many men say they want such a powerful force in their lives but may not be fully aware of all that comes with that reality. The ones, I suspect, who recognize the grace God has bestowed by sending such a competent mate use it as an opportunity to embrace all that she has to offer. I imagine such men value the type of women who challenge them, strengthen and elevate them, and help position them for victory, much like Aaron and Hur did for Moses. I imagine they recognize that such individuals are equipped to not only help them look or feel good, but to help them *be* good—becoming a better, higher version of themselves—becoming all that God has called them to be.

ESTHER

"Do not imagine that you in the king's palace can escape any more than all the other Jews. For if you keep silent at this time, liberation and rescue will arise for the Jews from another place, and you and your father's house will perish. And who knows whether you have not attained royalty for such a time as this?"
Esther 4:13–14

Wisdom in Scripture

We often talk about Esther, who was tasked with a noble mission to speak on behalf of her people to the king and to plead their case. She was ultimately placed in a position where she could uplift her people. It was a task she could have died for, but the words ring out in full force, what if you were brought to this place "for such a time as this?" (Esther 4:14). This place was one where she had been elevated to queen and, therefore, had access to the king that others did not have. This place was one where her people, the Jews, had been ordered to death by decree of the king. This place was one where her cousin, Mordecai, had been sentenced to the gallows through no fault of his own. This place harkens to one where many are brought to a point in life when God has called us to do something that may seem unreasonable, unsafe, or unimaginable. However, Esther had enough faith and courage to risk her life for her people, and it paid off in the end.

Esther spoke boldly to the king on behalf of her people, elevating their status in the king's eyes as she pleaded their case for life. In Esther 7:3, she said, "If I have found favor in your sight, O king, and it pleases the king, let my life be given me as my petition, and my people as my request; for we have been sold, I and my people, to be destroyed . . . " She spoke poignantly of the injustice that had been brought against her people, and the manner in which Haman, one of the king's officials, had manipulated the king to bring the plans to fruition. What better way to bring honor to your people than by giving voice to their plight, by highlighting the unjust threats against them, and bringing light to the actions of those empowered to bring them harm. She not only pleaded with the king to save the Jews' lives, but she was also able to save Mordecai, her cousin, from death and promoted him to a higher position in the kingdom. Her selflessness, resolute stance, and uncompromising faith uplifted those most precious to her, bringing honor to her family, her people, and the nation.

PROVERBS 31 WOMAN

She considers a field and buys it;
From her earnings she plants a vineyard.
She surrounds her waist with strength
And makes her arms strong.
She senses that her profit is good;
Her lamp does not go out at night.
She stretches out her hands to the distaff,
And her hands grasp the spindle.
She extends her hand to the poor,
And she stretches out her hands to the needy.
She is not afraid of the snow for her household,
For all her household are clothed with scarlet.
She makes coverings for herself;
Her clothing is fine linen and purple.
Her husband is known in the gates,
When he sits among the elders of the land.
She makes linen garments and sells them,
And supplies belts to the tradesmen.
Strength and dignity are her clothing,
And she smiles at the future.
She opens her mouth in wisdom,
And the teaching of kindness is on her tongue.
She watches over the activities of her household,
And does not eat the bread of idleness.
Her children rise up and bless her;
Her husband also, and he praises her, saying:
"Many daughters have done nobly,
But you excel them all."
Charm is deceitful and beauty is vain,
But a woman who fears the LORD, *she shall be praised.*
Proverbs 31:16–30

The book of Proverbs provides numerous examples of the role women can play in strengthening and uplifting those around them. To many, Proverbs showcases some of the most powerful descriptions of womanhood in the Bible. Proverbs 31:10 conveys the value of a good wife, asserting that " . . . her worth is far above jewels." Similarly, Proverbs 18:22 notes that a man who finds a wife "findeth" a good thing and gains the favor of God. "Findeth" denotes a continual state, a perpetual state of goodness. A woman of faith is even described as a crown to her husband. A crown is an adornment, something of great value that denotes respect, honor, and good standing. It speaks to the significance of having a woman of the highest quality who represents you well, one who will never bring shame or dishonor to the family, and one who will strengthen those around her through her insight and wisdom.

There is a simple but profound quote from Max Lucado suggesting that "God loves you just the way you are," but he loves you way too much "to leave you that way."[7] So many of us, I fear, never reach higher heights or become our best selves because we fail to surround ourselves with people who will push us to be all that God has called us to be, who will help strengthen us and our faith. A Godly woman, I contend, has the intuition and ability to bring out the best in those around her through living by example and pouring her wisdom into all she encounters.

The Proverbs 31 woman is often viewed as the prototype of Godly womanhood. She brought honor to her family by the way she lived, the way she carried herself, her resourcefulness, and her ingenuity in keeping her household running smoothly. She was the heart, the life force, and the soul of the family, keeping everything in place by the standards set by her wise counsel. Her husband and kids never had to worry that she would do anything to bring dishonor to the family because she was a woman of character and the best type of all, Godly character. I imagine she exuded God's grace and mercy, his patience, and his forgiveness. But most importantly, she exuded his love—a love that would never fail, a love that couldn't help but elevate and strengthen everyone in her circle and beyond.

LIVING ON PURPOSE

It is difficult to dismiss the incredible force a woman such as this can bring to her family and to the world. So often, when we read

7. Lucado, *Just Like Jesus*, 4.

Proverbs 31, we get fixated on all of the activities this woman was engaged in, her buying and selling goods, her making her family's clothing, and her giving to the needy and poor. All of these deeds are good but can seem overwhelming to achieve if you take these verses literally. As I have grown older, I realize all of the details matter much less than the spirit behind this woman's actions. The last sentence says it all, " . . . a woman who fears the LORD, she shall be praised" (Proverbs 31:30). Her respect for the leading of God and his sovereignty over her life motivated all of the previous actions. Her considering a field and buying it represents her willingness to invest the resources God entrusted to her to bring about a harvest of blessings for her family, signified by the "vineyard." Her making clothing for the household and providing for the poor represents her desire to meet the needs of all those around her, a calling stirred by the loving actions of God himself. The reason she "smiles at the future" and is covered in "strength and dignity" is because she has put all of her faith and trust in God, who she recognizes has all power and control. And finally, the reason she "opens her mouth in wisdom" and teaches love and kindness is because she believes God and what his Word proclaims, recognizing the beauty and necessity of everyone embracing and embodying his teachings.

It is hard to deny this type of woman's influence in representing God's will in spaces often devoid of any spiritual awareness or aptitude. Her example, her tenacity, her dedication to a calling above self, and a life marked by devotion to fulfilling the Creator's plans over her own, is one maybe we should all seek to replicate. Perhaps, like the Proverbs 31 woman, it is incumbent upon us as *ezer* women to consider adorning ourselves with love, reverence, and commitment to God and all that he represents so we can motivate those around us to aim higher—to reach for higher heights, a higher calling, and a higher purpose.

Questions to Consider:

1. Describe a time when you uplifted or strengthened someone close to you. How was it similar or different from the example of Aaron and Hur strengthening Moses in Exodus 17?

2. Are there times you brought honor or a higher standing to those around you due to your behavior and example? If so, explain. Is this representative of the way God strengthens and elevates his people? If so, in what way? If not, why?

3. Is there a character, male or female, in the Bible that you identify with most that represents how you uplifted or strengthened someone?

4. If God has entrusted you with this power or gift, how can you use it best to bring him glory?

Walking in Wisdom

God calls us all to higher altitudes.
Let us create a space where others are
uplifted, encouraging them
to grow and elevate to achieve their God-given purpose.

CHAPTER 10

Answering the Call

Embracing Our Collective Power

*"She will be his strongest ally in pursuing God's purposes
and his first roadblock when he veers off course."*[1]

—CAROLYN CUSTIS JAMES

ON DECEMBER 29, 2024, the thirty-ninth president of the United States, James Earl Carter Jr., better known as Jimmy Carter, passed away at the age of one hundred. He became president the year of my birth, and being a native of Georgia, he always held a special place in my heart compared to all the other presidents. As political scholars often assert, he was not considered a particularly successful president, only serving one term, but he experienced perhaps his best successes outside of the political arena. Of course, he enhanced diplomatic relations with numerous countries, promoted peace and human rights throughout the world, and won the Nobel Peace Prize for his efforts. And although he served proudly as State Senator and Governor of Georgia, followed by President of the United States, when asked in 2015 what his most profound achievement was, he spoke only of building and cultivating a

1. James, *Half the Church.*

96

wonderful union with his partner Rosalynn. After seventy-seven years of marriage, four children, twelve grandchildren, and fourteen great-grandchildren, upon her death, he described her in this way: "Rosalynn was my equal partner in everything I ever accomplished. She gave me wise guidance and encouragement when I needed it. As long as Rosalynn was in the world, I always knew somebody loved and supported me."[2]

He credited their biggest success as a couple to his being elected to the presidency with what he called Rosalynn's "good help."[3] Rosalynn was, by many estimates, the quiet force in his life that made the most profound impact on him personally and professionally. Equal partner, wise guidance, encouragement, support, good help—these words sound familiar, don't they? I believe Carter's words hearken to the very essence of the term *ezer*, representing the sentiment expressed by Adam's declaration the day Eve was presented to him in the garden (Genesis 2:23). Adam exclaimed, "At last this is bone of my bones, and flesh of my flesh ... " These words signified a supreme credit and gratitude for what the Creator had supplied—the provision of exactly what he needed precisely when he needed it most—a companion suited for him, equipped to strengthen and aid him in carrying out God's plans.[4]

Perhaps Carter understood that women were not created to simply serve or assist men in fulfilling their mission, but instead to work alongside them as an indelible force and unquestionable asset in reaching common goals. Maybe he recognized that women represented a much-welcomed source of aid, and thus, warranted an eager expectancy and overwhelming appreciation for their presence. Perhaps, likewise, we too should consider the necessity of such support in completing a mission God never intended to be accomplished by man alone. When we consider this notion, we must also ponder whether restoring and embracing *ezer* requires effort on both men's and women's parts. While women are adopting a deeper understanding of how to live out their *ezer* nature,

2. Carter, "Former First Lady Rosalynn."
3. Epstein, "Jimmy and Rosalynn."
4. Matthews, "God Created Woman."

men, perhaps, in turn, must embrace greater acknowledgement and appreciation of women's true value and strength. Only when both occur can God's purpose for creating Eve in the garden so many years ago be truly fulfilled and truly realized.

I believe the inspired words in scripture are not written by chance or happenstance, that God does not speak in hollow or feckless terms. I believe his word is a clarion call for all of us to heed. What if God is calling women to a greater fulfillment of their purpose, as exemplified through embodying their *ezer* nature, while simultaneously calling men to fulfill their unique purpose, including nurturing and cultivating women's gifts so that God's plans are ultimately achieved? Conceivably, this is one of the reasons God commands men to "love their wives as Christ also loved the church and gave Himself up for her" (Ephesians 5:25). Maybe this is why he encourages men to "show her honor as a fellow heir of the grace of life, so that your prayers will not be hindered" (1 Peter 3:7). What if men and women's spiritual success is inextricably tied? What if honoring and uplifting each one's unique gifts leads to a win-win situation for all? The result would be that women and men both show up in their fullness, realizing that they are better able to accomplish the assignments God has given them through their shared spirit and action.

I wonder what we could accomplish if we ultimately seek to have what Paul equates to a Christ mindset, " . . . maintaining the same love, united in spirit, intent on one purpose" (Philippians 2:2). Maybe what God truly calls us to is a mentality where the intent is not simply to assert our own importance, to seek our own will, or to even accomplish greatness on an island all by ourselves. But maybe the goal is that we recognize we can achieve so much more together, so it behooves us to exhort and build one another up so that we all become what God originally intended at Creation. Then, collectively, we can work in tandem to help bring to fruition God's perfect plans, the reconciling of mankind back to Him. God, the ultimate *ezer*, our consummate help, is perhaps summoning us all to answer the call. So, "let's hold firmly to the confession of our hope without wavering . . . and let's consider how to encourage one another in love and good deeds . . ." (Hebrews 10:23–25). Then we can get back to being what God intended in the beginning.

Selah

Walking in Wisdom

Let us remain united in love, spirit, and purpose,
knowing that we can accomplish far more together than apart.

Afterword

Be very careful . . . how you live—not as unwise
but as wise, making the most of every opportunity,
because the days are evil. Therefore, do not be
foolish, but understand what the Lord's will is.

EPHESIANS 5:15–17 NIV

TO MY BEAUTIFUL *EZER* mother,

On September 16, 2008, God gifted me with you, a wonderful woman whose eyes sparkled with hope and whose warm embrace cradled my beginnings. Your warm presence whispered of the unwavering love that I would carry with me all my years. Ever since I can remember, I have grown up in this fantasy world, protected and nurtured by the one who selflessly put me first. You brought me into a world defined by harsh societal norms, a world flooded with obstacles and boundaries of all kinds, yet you fostered within me a boundless imagination, and you cultivated a safe space where your deep love would mold me into a purposeful woman led by God's everlasting peace, strength, and love. This deep love that you have for both me and my brother allows us to walk unapologetically, seeking the LORD who blessed us with the strongest woman we know.

Although we once questioned your overprotective ways, especially the television shows that we weren't allowed to watch or the songs that went unheard, we now realize that it was all to protect us from the quiet, yet wicked ways the world tries to brainwash society. Despite the world's attempt, because of your guidance, we are able to find our identity in God, which allows us to counter what the world deems as normal. God's love is indeed reflected in you. I am truly amazed by how you treat every soul you come in contact with, no matter whether you're in a good or bad mood, with compassion and care as you exhibit the fruits of the spirit. I recognize now the source of this spirit.

While writing and conducting research for this book, I quickly began to understand the importance of people's stories. Your story is what has molded you into the wonderful being you are. It's like the gentle brush strokes of a soft paintbrush across an empty canvas, each stroke and the resulting marks gradually, over time, resemble the fullness of an art piece. It's like a flower blooming in early Spring, starting from its strong, rooted foundation, blossoming into something so beautiful, shaped by its nourishing surroundings. Through the interviews I conducted, I discovered many things about our family and particularly your mother's life. As I grew in deepening love and was moved by Granny's story, it motivated me to dive even deeper into learning more about her history and bringing her past to light. I learned about how her upbringing greatly influenced who she is today. Her adopted family, taking her and her siblings in, shaped her caring and empathetic spirit. She brought this spirit into her career, marriage, and into her relationships with you, your sister, and her grandchildren, leaving a lasting legacy of compassion, faith, and love for all to see.

He must increase, but I must decrease.
John 3:30

What I have learned most from Granny and your echoing footsteps is that I must surrender to God so that I can be available to him, allowing him to use me for his greater purpose. Mom, countless times I watch you willingly surrender your passions, time, and heart to the Lord, which inspires me to do the same. When I become less under God, I realize that this life isn't about my desires, but it's all about God's purpose. No destiny is for my personal applause or individual gain, and once I understand this fact, I am able to rest on his promises confidently regarding the future ahead of me. When I give up control, I can feel God's presence and experience his unwavering love, hope, and goodness more clearly. The peace, love, and joy that we inherit from God surpasses all understanding, and it is through my weakness that it shows up the most.

As I walk and watch the days of my life unfold, I become more aware of the troubles and hardships that you can't hide from. Yes, the pain from your struggles can hurt, but the struggles are necessary. I've learned that through my suffering, God sometimes purposefully makes me smaller so I can depend on him more fully, but when I go through the struggles of life, God will never leave me, but instead, he walks with me through the pain even though he sees the beautiful future and joy that lies on the other side.

From your example, Mom, I understand not to be mad at God when he allows us to go through seasons of distress because the valley is where the most beautiful flowers grow, and when I elevate to the mountaintop, all the glory is given to him because he prepared me for that very moment. I can only elevate through God's grace, by internalizing his voice, which I hear more clearly when I give my life to him.

For the past sixteen years of my life, you have been my guiding force. I watch as you step into every situation with grace, and you lead with strength, deep wisdom, and most importantly, love. You have shaped the way I view the world, and you serve as a vessel using your words to spread the truth. You stepping into your light gives me, along with many other women all over the world, permission to do the same. I love you.

—Your favorite daughter!

"Let your heart take hold of my words;
Keep my commandments and live;
Acquire wisdom! Acquire understanding!
Do not forget nor turn away from the words of my mouth.
Do not abandon her, and she will guard you;
Love her, and she will watch over you.
The beginning of wisdom is: Acquire wisdom;
And with all your possessions, acquire understanding.
Prize her, and she will exalt you;
She will honor you if you embrace her.
She will place on your head a garland of grace;
She will present you with a crown of beauty."
Proverbs 4:4–9

Appendix

Supplemental Discussion Questions
for Teens and Young Adults

GOD'S WISDOM AND PROVISION:

1. How would you define wisdom? What is Godly wisdom?

2. How important do you think wisdom is when it comes to decision-making (e.g., choosing friends, college decisions, dating)? How have you used wisdom when making life decisions?

3. Do you agree with the statement that "God gives us what we need when we need it most"? Why or why not? If so, describe examples of this happening in your life.

WOMEN AND SOCIETY:

1. How do you feel about the way women have been portrayed in tv, film, and music? Provide examples of what you like or dislike.

2. Who do you consider to be the most popular examples or images of womanhood in today's tv, film, and music? What do their examples say about the world's view of womanhood?

3. How do the images in tv, film, and music compare to how God describes women in the Bible?

4. Why do you think women don't have a more prominent role as superhero characters and how might that mimic the way women act and are treated in society today?

5. In an era of social media (e.g., TikTok, Instagram) and reality tv how difficult is it to be a woman of faith? Where do you find examples of faithful women?

PURPOSE AND POWER:

1. Why is it important that we don't let the things of this world (e.g., materialism, media images) be the source of our strength, fulfillment, and purpose?

2. What are some things we can do that allow us to hear God's voice clearer which further strengthens our alignment with his will and purpose? What are some ways you can practice hearing God's voice?

3. Do you believe most teenage girls and young women are aware of their value and power? Do you believe they exercise that power?

4. A lot of times life almost feels rushed, like we're always chasing the next best thing without being grateful for our successes in the present moment. Social media and other images cause us to compare where we are to other people's accomplishments. Do you think God wants us to compare ourselves to others? Why or why not? How do we practice being grateful for the blessings God has provided in our lives?

5. Chapter 4 suggests our love of superheroes may stem from a longing for the true Savior. What things in your life do you make your "savior" even subconsciously? Do you find yourself constantly longing to be saved by the people and things of this world?

LIVING OUR EZER NATURE:

1. How can we as teenage girls and young women exemplify *ezer* qualities in the world we live in today?

2. Why is it so important to use and nurture the gifts God gives us instead of neglecting them?

3. Isn't it interesting how the Bible uses the term *ezer* to describe God's strength and great helping power, but it also relates to women. This directly counters the world's distorted view. What does this tell you about where we should place our worth?

4. Why is it so important to treat others with the same selfless and sincere love that Jesus gives to us?

5. What are some ways we can actively love others more like Jesus? How do we do this, even though society glamorizes and glorifies self-love or putting yourself first in every situation no matter what?

6. What are some ways you have provided emotional support and relief to those around you?

7. What are some ways we can guard and protect what is of value to God?

8. In what ways can we uplift and encourage people that we might not like?

9. How can others seeing us abiding in God and growing spiritually inspire them to also want to grow?

10. How can having friendships rooted in Christ naturally uplift us?

Bibliography

Baxter, Mary. "Priscilla—Acts 18." Blue Letter Bible, last modified March 7, 2011. https://www.blueletterbible.org/Comm/baxter_mary/WitW/WitW50_Priscilla.cfm.

Carter, James. "Former First Lady Rosalynn Carter Passes Away at Age 96." Statement from the Carter Center, November 19, 2023.

Chang, Rachel. "Coretta Scott King and Betty Shabazz Formed an Unbreakable Bond After Their Husbands's Tragic Deaths." Hearst Magazine Media, Inc., January 6, 2021. https://www.biography.com/activists/a64242047/betty-shabazz-coretta-scott-king-bond.

Combe, Rachael. "At the Pinnacle of Hillary Clinton's Career." *Elle*, April 5, 2012. https://www.elle.com/culture/career-politics/interviews/a12529/at-the-pinnacle-of-hillary-clintons-career-654140/.

Darrow, Jessica. "Surface Pressure." *Encanto (Original Motion Picture Soundtrack)*. Lin-Manuel Miranda. Track 3. Walt Disney Records, 2021.

Epstein, Kayla. "Jimmy and Rosalynn Carter's Legendary 77-Year Marriage." BBC News, December 30, 2024.

Fisher, Sarah. "Helper: Defining the Ezer Woman." *Hebrew Word Lessons*, May 13, 2018. www.hebrewwordlessons.com.

Georgetown Institute for Women, Peace, and Security. *Seeking Peace* podcast. "Malala Yousafzai's Dad on the Importance of Girls' Education." https://www.giwps.georgetown.edu.

Gilbert, Larry. *Team Ministry: Gifted to Serve*. Church Growth Institute, 2014.

Guzik, David. "Study Guide for Genesis 2." Blue Letter Bible, last modified June 2022. https://www.blueletterbible.org/comm/guzik_david/study-guide/genesis/genesis-2.cfm.

———. "Study Guide for 2 Kings 5." Blue Letter Bible, last modified August 2002. https://www.blueletterbible.org/comm/guzik_david/study-guide/2-kings/2-kings-5.cfm?a=318005.

———. "Study Guide for Matthew 22." Blue Letter Bible, last modified June 2022. https://www.blueletterbible.org/comm/guzik_david/study-guide/matthew/matthew-22.cfm.

———. "Study Guide for Philippians 2." Blue Letter Bible, last modified June 2022. https://www.blueletterbible.org/comm/guzik_david/study-guide/philippians/philippians-2.cfm.

———. "Study Guide for 1 Timothy 2." Blue Letter Bible, last modified June 2022. https://www.blueletterbible.org/comm/guzik_david/study-guide/1-timothy/1-timothy-2.cfm.

Harrell, Michelle. *I Am Ezer: The Glory of a Woman*. Christian Faith, 2023.

Henry, Matthew. "Commentary on Matthew 22." Blue Letter Bible, last modified March 1, 1996. https://www.blueletterbible.org/Comm/mhc/Mat/Mat_022.cfm.

Hobbs, Lottie B. *Daughters of Eve*. Fort Worth: Harvest Publications, 1963.

Hodge, Jill, host. Episode 48, "Mother Teresa on Doing Small Things with Great Love." February 12, 2025. Podcast. https://www.lettheverseflow.com/mother-teresa-doing-small-things-with-great-love/.

James, Carolyn C. *Half the Church: Recapturing God's Global Vision for Women*. Grand Rapids: Zondervan, 2010.

Jia, Haomiao, and Erica I. Lubetkin. "Life Expectancy and Active Life Expectancy by Marital Status Among Older U.S. Adults: Results from the U.S. Medicare Health Outcome Survey." *SSM Population Health*. August 15, 2020.

Jones, Rachel. "The Warriors of This West African Kingdom Were Formidable—and Female." *National Geographic*, September 14, 2022.

King, Martin Luther Jr. "Loving Your Enemies." Speech, Dexter Avenue Baptist Church, Montgomery, AL, November 17, 1957. www.gardnerkansas.gov.

Long, Everett, Monica Ponder, and Stephanie Bernard. "Knowledge, Attitudes, and Beliefs Related to Hypertension and Hyperlipidemia Self-Management Among African-American Men Living in the Southeastern United States." *Patient Education and Counseling*, vol. 100, no. 5 (2017): 1000–1006.

Longhurst, Erin N. *Omoiyari: The Japanese Art of Compassion*. New York: Harper Collins, 2020.

Lucado, Max. *Just Like Jesus*. Word Publishing, 1998.

Matthews, Alice. "God Created Woman as an *Ezer* Kind of Helper." Theology of Work Project, Inc. www.theologyofwork.org, February 4, 2017.

Mckesson, Deray (@iamderay). "Don't Settle for Happiness," Instagram, September 7, 2025. https://www.instagram.com/ reel/DOgWqCfjd3z/

Mixed Martial Arts Conditioning Association. "The Complete History of Judo: From Ancient Japan to Modern Martial Arts." https://mixedmartialartsconditioningassociation.com, September 20, 2023.

Obama, Michelle. "Democratic National Convention (speech)." Philadelphia, PA, July 25, 2016.

Pinckney, James. "You Fight On." *The Sound of Holiness*. James F. Pinckney Jr. Track 5. OPHIRGOSPEL, 2020.

Reuters. "Grieving Chimpanzee Carries Dead Baby for Months at Spanish Zoo." Reuters News, May 21, 2024. https://www.reuters.com.

Starlin, Jim. "Dr. Strange," *Marvel Shadows & Light*, no. 2. Marvel Comics, 1998.

Strong, James. *Strong's Expanded Exhaustive Concordance of the Bible*. Hendrickson Academic, 2009, s.v. "help meet" (H5828).

———. *Strong's Expanded Exhaustive Concordance of the Bible*. Hendrickson Academic, 2009, s.v. "*neged*" (H5048).

U.S. Attorney's Office for the Southern District of New York. "Sean Combs Charged in Manhattan Federal Court with Sex Trafficking and Other Federal Offenses." Press release, September 17, 2024, https://www.justice.gov/usao-sdny/pr/sean-combs-charged-manhattan-federal-court-sex-trafficking-and-other-federal-offenses.

Yousafzai, Malala. *I Am Malala: The Girl Who Stood Up for Education and Was Shot by the Taliban*. New York: Little, Brown and Company, 2013.

———. "United Nations Speech on Youth Education," Archives of Women's Political Communication, Iowa State University, July 12, 2013. www.awpc.cattcenter.iastate.edu.